# TEACHER'S PET PUBLICATIONS

PUZZLE PACK
for
The House on Mango Street

based on the book by
Sandra Cisneros

Written by
William T. Collins

© 2005 Teacher's Pet Publications
All Rights Reserved

The materials in this packet are copyrighted
by Teacher's Pet Publications, Inc.

These pages may be duplicated by the purchaser
for use in the purchaser's own classroom.

Copying any of these materials and distributing them
for any other purpose is a violation of the copyright laws.

© 2005 Teacher's Pet Publications, Inc.
www.tpet.com

INTRODUCTION
If you already own the LitPlan for this title, this Puzzle Pack will refresh your Unit Resource Materials and Vocabulary Resource Materials sections plus give you additional materials you can substitute into the tests. If you do not already have a complete LitPlan, these pages will give you some supplemental materials to use with your own plan. There are two main groups of materials: one set for unit words (such as characters' names, symbols, places, etc.) and one set for vocabulary words associated with the book.

WORD LIST
There is a word list for both the unit words and the vocabulary words. These lists show you which words are being used in the materials and the clues or definitions being used for those words. You may want to give students a word list with clues/definitions to help them, or you may want students to only have a word list (without clues/definitions) if you want them to work a little harder. Both are available for duplication. The word lists can also be your "calling key" for the bingo games.

FILL IN THE BLANK AND MATCHING
There are 4 each of the fill in the blank and matching worksheets for both the unit and vocabulary words. These pages can be used either as extra worksheets for students or as objective parts of a unit test. They can be done individually if students need extra help or as a whole class activity to review the material covered.

MAGIC SQUARES
The magic squares not only reinforce the material covered but also work on reasoning and math skills. Many teachers have told us that their students really enjoy doing these!

WORD SEARCH PUZZLES
The word search words go in all directions, as indicated on your answer keys. Two of the word search puzzles have the clues listed rather than the words. This makes the puzzle a little more difficult, but it reinforces the material better. Two word search puzzles have words only for students who find the clue puzzles too difficult.

CROSSWORD PUZZLES
Both unit and vocabulary word sections have 4 crossword puzzles.

BINGO CARDS
There are 32 individual bingo cards for the unit words and 32 individual bingo cards for the vocabulary words. You can use your word list as a "call list," calling the words at random and marking them off of your list as you go, or you could use the flash cards by cutting them apart and drawing the words at random from a hat (or box or whatever). To make a better review, you might ask for the definition and spelling of each word as you call it out–or you could call out the definitions and have students tell you the words they need to look for on the puzzle.

JUGGLE LETTERS
The vocabulary juggle letter game is intended to help students learn the spellings of the words. One sheet has the definitions listed on it as an extra help for students who need it or to reinforce the definitions if you choose to do so.

FLASH CARDS
We've included a set of vocabulary flash cards you can duplicate, cut, and fold for your students. Some teachers make a few sets for general use by the class; others make a set for each student. Some teachers duplicate them for each student and have the students cut & fold their own. You can cut out just the words and put them in a hat, have each student pick out one word and write the definition and a sentence for that word. Students then swap words and papers, with the next student adding a sentence of his own under the last one. You can have students swap as many times as you like. Each time the student will read the sentences written prior to his own and then add a sentence. You can cut out the words and definitions separately and play "I Have; Who Has?" Each student in the room draws a word and definition. The first student says, "I have (the name of the word). Who has the definition?" The student with the definition reads it then says, "I have (the name of the vocabulary word she has). Who has the definition?" The round continues until all words and definitions have been given.

House on Mango Street Unit Word List

No.	Word	Clue/Definition
1.	ALICIA	Is afraid of mice
2.	BABY	The ____ Boy; sings Pepsi commercials
3.	BENNY	Mr. ____; grocery store owner
4.	BIKE	Esperanza chipped in to buy it
5.	BOBO	Ruthie's dog
6.	BUICK	Esperanza compares her hips to one
7.	CADILLAC	Type of car Louie's cousin steals
8.	CANTEEN	Esperanza wants to eat there
9.	CATHY	Says the neighborhood is getting bad
10.	CORDERO	Esperanza's last name
11.	DARIUS	Says a cloud was God
12.	DAVEY	His brother has a crooked eye
13.	EARL	Kids don't agree on what his wife looks like
14.	EDNA	Ruthie's mother
15.	ELENITA	Tells fortunes with cards
16.	ESPERANZA	Likes to tell stories
17.	GERALDO	Dies in hit and run accident
18.	GIL	Owner of the used furniture store
19.	GRANDMOTHER	Great-____; Esperanza is named for her
20.	HEELS	High ____; a woman gives some to the girls to play with
21.	HORSE	Chinese year of Esperanza's birth
22.	KEELER	Home street between Paulina and Loomis
23.	LOIS	Sire's girlfriend
24.	LOOMIS	Home between Mango and Keeler
25.	LUCY	The big sister, born in Texas
26.	LUPE	Aunt ____; died the day the girls made fun of her
27.	MAGDALENA	Nenny's real name
28.	MAMACITA	Sits by the window and plays the Spanish radio
29.	MANGO	The family owns the house here
30.	MARIN	Louie's cousin who sells Avon
31.	MEME	Won the contest and broke both arms
32.	MEXICAN	____-American; Esperanza's nationality
33.	MINERVA	Writes poems at night
34.	MONKEY	____ Garden; kids go there to play
35.	MUSIC	____ Box; made Esperanza feel stupid
36.	NACHO	Uncle ____; dances with Esperanza
37.	NENNY	Younger sister to Esperanza
38.	PAULINA	Home before Keller
39.	PUERTO	____ Rican; Marin's nationality
40.	RACHEL	The little sister, born in Chicago
41.	RAFAELA	Likes to drink coconut and papaya juices
42.	ROSA	____ Vargas; has too many children
43.	RUTHIE	Adult who likes to play
44.	SALLY	Wants to love and love
45.	SIRE	Esperanza noticed him looking at her
46.	SISTERS	Three ____ told Esperanza to come back to Mango Street
47.	TREES	The only ones who understand Esperanza
48.	VARGAS	Angel ____; tried to fly and dropped from the sky
49.	ZEZE	____ The X; the name Esperanza wants

House on Mango Street Fill In The Blank 1

_____

1. Chinese year of Esperanza's birth
2. Says the neighborhood is getting bad
3. The family owns the house here
4. The only ones who understand Esperanza
5. Aunt ____; died the day the girls made fun of her
6. Owner of the used furniture store
7. Mr. ____; grocery store owner
8. Home between Mango and Keeler
9. Ruthie's dog
10. Says a cloud was God
11. Esperanza compares her hips to one
12. Younger sister to Esperanza
13. Esperanza noticed him looking at her
14. ____ Rican; Marin's nationality
15. Esperanza wants to eat there
16. ____ Vargas; has too many children
17. ____ Garden; kids go there to play
18. Three ____ told Esperanza to come back to Mango Street
19. Likes to drink coconut and papaya juices
20. Kids don't agree on what his wife looks like

House on Mango Street Fill in The Blank 1 Answer Key

HORSE	1. Chinese year of Esperanza's birth
CATHY	2. Says the neighborhood is getting bad
MANGO	3. The family owns the house here
TREES	4. The only ones who understand Esperanza
LUPE	5. Aunt ____; died the day the girls made fun of her
GIL	6. Owner of the used furniture store
BENNY	7. Mr. ____; grocery store owner
LOOMIS	8. Home between Mango and Keeler
BOBO	9. Ruthie's dog
DARIUS	10. Says a cloud was God
BUICK	11. Esperanza compares her hips to one
NENNY	12. Younger sister to Esperanza
SIRE	13. Esperanza noticed him looking at her
PUERTO	14. ____ Rican; Marin's nationality
CANTEEN	15. Esperanza wants to eat there
ROSA	16. ____ Vargas; has too many children
MONKEY	17. ____ Garden; kids go there to play
SISTERS	18. Three ____ told Esperanza to come back to Mango Street
RAFAELA	19. Likes to drink coconut and papaya juices
EARL	20. Kids don't agree on what his wife looks like

House on Mango Street Fill In The Blank 2

_____

_____

_____

_____

_____

_____

_____

_____

_____

_____

_____

_____

_____

_____

_____

_____

_____

_____

_____

_____

1. Esperanza wants to eat there
2. Angel ____ ; tried to fly and dropped from the sky
3. Sits by the window and plays the Spanish radio
4. Chinese year of Esperanza's birth
5. ____ Vargas; has too many children
6. ____ The X; the name Esperanza wants
7. Mr. ____; grocery store owner
8. Louie's cousin who sells Avon
9. Esperanza chipped in to buy it
10. His brother has a crooked eye
11. ____-American; Esperanza's nationality
12. Three ____ told Esperanza to come back to Mango Street
13. Says a cloud was God
14. Esperanza compares her hips to one
15. The only ones who understand Esperanza
16. Likes to tell stories
17. Uncle ____; dances with Esperanza
18. The little sister, born in Chicago
19. Esperanza noticed him looking at her
20. ____ Rican; Marin's nationality

House on Mango Street Fill In The Blank 2 Answer Key

Answer	Clue
CANTEEN	1. Esperanza wants to eat there
VARGAS	2. Angel ____ ; tried to fly and dropped from the sky
MAMACITA	3. Sits by the window and plays the Spanish radio
HORSE	4. Chinese year of Esperanza's birth
ROSA	5. ____ Vargas; has too many children
ZEZE	6. ____ The X; the name Esperanza wants
BENNY	7. Mr. ____; grocery store owner
MARIN	8. Louie's cousin who sells Avon
BIKE	9. Esperanza chipped in to buy it
DAVEY	10. His brother has a crooked eye
MEXICAN	11. ____-American; Esperanza's nationality
SISTERS	12. Three ____ told Esperanza to come back to Mango Street
DARIUS	13. Says a cloud was God
BUICK	14. Esperanza compares her hips to one
TREES	15. The only ones who understand Esperanza
ESPERANZA	16. Likes to tell stories
NACHO	17. Uncle ____; dances with Esperanza
RACHEL	18. The little sister, born in Chicago
SIRE	19. Esperanza noticed him looking at her
PUERTO	20. ____ Rican; Marin's nationality

House on Mango Street Fill In The Blank 3

_____

1. The little sister, born in Chicago
2. Sire's girlfriend
3. The family owns the house here
4. Kids don't agree on what his wife looks like
5. ____ Box; made Esperanza feel stupid
6. His brother has a crooked eye
7. Ruthie's mother
8. Angel ____; tried to fly and dropped from the sky
9. The ____ Boy; sings Pepsi commercials
10. Great-____; Esperanza is named for her
11. Won the contest and broke both arms
12. Is afraid of mice
13. ____-American; Esperanza's nationality
14. Says the neighborhood is getting bad
15. Mr. ____; grocery store owner
16. Says a cloud was God
17. ____ Vargas; has too many children
18. Home between Mango and Keeler
19. Three ____ told Esperanza to come back to Mango Street
20. Sits by the window and plays the Spanish radio

House on Mango Street Fill In The Blank 3 Answer Key

RACHEL	1. The little sister, born in Chicago
LOIS	2. Sire's girlfriend
MANGO	3. The family owns the house here
EARL	4. Kids don't agree on what his wife looks like
MUSIC	5. ____ Box; made Esperanza feel stupid
DAVEY	6. His brother has a crooked eye
EDNA	7. Ruthie's mother
VARGAS	8. Angel ____ ; tried to fly and dropped from the sky
BABY	9. The ____ Boy; sings Pepsi commercials
GRANDMOTHER	10. Great-____; Esperanza is named for her
MEME	11. Won the contest and broke both arms
ALICIA	12. Is afraid of mice
MEXICAN	13. ____-American; Esperanza's nationality
CATHY	14. Says the neighborhood is getting bad
BENNY	15. Mr. ____; grocery store owner
DARIUS	16. Says a cloud was God
ROSA	17. ____ Vargas; has too many children
LOOMIS	18. Home between Mango and Keeler
SISTERS	19. Three ____ told Esperanza to come back to Mango Street
MAMACITA	20. Sits by the window and plays the Spanish radio

House on Mango Street Fill in The Blank 4

_____ 1. Esperanza noticed him looking at her

_____ 2. Wants to love and love

_____ 3. Esperanza's last name

_____ 4. ____ Garden; kids go there to play

_____ 5. Is afraid of mice

_____ 6. Says the neighborhood is getting bad

_____ 7. ____ The X; the name Esperanza wants

_____ 8. Mr. ____; grocery store owner

_____ 9. Likes to drink coconut and papaya juices

_____ 10. The only ones who understand Esperanza

_____ 11. High ____; a woman gives some to the girls to play with

_____ 12. Sits by the window and plays the Spanish radio

_____ 13. Home street between Paulina and Loomis

_____ 14. Nenny's real name

_____ 15. ____ Rican; Marin's nationality

_____ 16. Home before Keller

_____ 17. Chinese year of Esperanza's birth

_____ 18. Likes to tell stories

_____ 19. Dies in hit and run accident

_____ 20. ____-American; Esperanza's nationality

House on Mango Street Fill In The Blank 4 Answer Key

SIRE	1. Esperanza noticed him looking at her
SALLY	2. Wants to love and love
CORDERO	3. Esperanza's last name
MONKEY	4. ____ Garden; kids go there to play
ALICIA	5. Is afraid of mice
CATHY	6. Says the neighborhood is getting bad
ZEZE	7. ____ The X; the name Esperanza wants
BENNY	8. Mr. ____; grocery store owner
RAFAELA	9. Likes to drink coconut and papaya juices
TREES	10. The only ones who understand Esperanza
HEELS	11. High ____; a woman gives some to the girls to play with
MAMACITA	12. Sits by the window and plays the Spanish radio
KEELER	13. Home street between Paulina and Loomis
MAGDALENA	14. Nenny's real name
PUERTO	15. ____ Rican; Marin's nationality
PAULINA	16. Home before Keller
HORSE	17. Chinese year of Esperanza's birth
ESPERANZA	18. Likes to tell stories
GERALDO	19. Dies in hit and run accident
MEXICAN	20. ____-American; Esperanza's nationality

House on Mango Street Matching 1

___ 1. MARIN A. Home between Mango and Keeler
___ 2. MUSIC B. Esperanza chipped in to buy it
___ 3. RUTHIE C. Esperanza noticed him looking at her
___ 4. LUCY D. ____ Box; made Esperanza feel stupid
___ 5. SIRE E. Tells fortunes with cards
___ 6. MANGO F. Esperanza wants to eat there
___ 7. MAMACITA G. Louie's cousin who sells Avon
___ 8. GERALDO H. The family owns the house here
___ 9. SISTERS I. Writes poems at night
___10. DAVEY J. ____ The X; the name Esperanza wants
___11. EDNA K. Says a cloud was God
___12. MONKEY L. Ruthie's mother
___13. BENNY M. His brother has a crooked eye
___14. ALICIA N. Dies in hit and run accident
___15. ELENITA O. Great-____; Esperanza is named for her
___16. NACHO P. The big sister, born in Texas
___17. GRANDMOTHER Q. Adult who likes to play
___18. LOOMIS R. Mr. ____; grocery store owner
___19. CANTEEN S. Is afraid of mice
___20. DARIUS T. Esperanza's last name
___21. BUICK U. ____ Garden; kids go there to play
___22. CORDERO V. Esperanza compares her hips to one
___23. ZEZE W. Three ____ told Esperanza to come back to Mango Street
___24. BIKE X. Uncle ____; dances with Esperanza
___25. MINERVA Y. Sits by the window and plays the Spanish radio

House on Mango Street Matching 1 Answer Key

G - 1. MARIN	A.	Home between Mango and Keeler
D - 2. MUSIC	B.	Esperanza chipped in to buy it
Q - 3. RUTHIE	C.	Esperanza noticed him looking at her
P - 4. LUCY	D.	____ Box; made Esperanza feel stupid
C - 5. SIRE	E.	Tells fortunes with cards
H - 6. MANGO	F.	Esperanza wants to eat there
Y - 7. MAMACITA	G.	Louie's cousin who sells Avon
N - 8. GERALDO	H.	The family owns the house here
W - 9. SISTERS	I.	Writes poems at night
M -10. DAVEY	J.	____ The X; the name Esperanza wants
L -11. EDNA	K.	Says a cloud was God
U -12. MONKEY	L.	Ruthie's mother
R -13. BENNY	M.	His brother has a crooked eye
S -14. ALICIA	N.	Dies in hit and run accident
E -15. ELENITA	O.	Great-____; Esperanza is named for her
X -16. NACHO	P.	The big sister, born in Texas
O -17. GRANDMOTHER	Q.	Adult who likes to play
A -18. LOOMIS	R.	Mr. ____; grocery store owner
F -19. CANTEEN	S.	Is afraid of mice
K -20. DARIUS	T.	Esperanza's last name
V -21. BUICK	U.	____ Garden; kids go there to play
T -22. CORDERO	V.	Esperanza compares her hips to one
J -23. ZEZE	W.	Three ____ told Esperanza to come back to Mango Street
B -24. BIKE	X.	Uncle ____; dances with Esperanza
I -25. MINERVA	Y.	Sits by the window and plays the Spanish radio

House on Mango Street Matching 2

___ 1. PAULINA   A. ____ Garden; kids go there to play
___ 2. VARGAS   B. Dies in hit and run accident
___ 3. ESPERANZA   C. The little sister, born in Chicago
___ 4. BOBO   D. Wants to love and love
___ 5. HEELS   E. Home between Mango and Keeler
___ 6. ZEZE   F. Esperanza wants to eat there
___ 7. LUCY   G. Likes to tell stories
___ 8. ROSA   H. Type of car Louie's cousin steals
___ 9. EDNA   I. High ____; a woman gives some to the girls to play with
___10. EARL   J. Writes poems at night
___11. CADILLAC   K. The ____ Boy; sings Pepsi commercials
___12. RUTHIE   L. ____ The X; the name Esperanza wants
___13. ALICIA   M. Ruthie's mother
___14. KEELER   N. Home street between Paulina and Loomis
___15. RACHEL   O. Is afraid of mice
___16. CANTEEN   P. Likes to drink coconut and papaya juices
___17. LOOMIS   Q. Great-____; Esperanza is named for her
___18. SALLY   R. Ruthie's dog
___19. MINERVA   S. Angel ____ ; tried to fly and dropped from the sky
___20. BABY   T. Adult who likes to play
___21. MONKEY   U. Home before Keller
___22. GERALDO   V. Kids don't agree on what his wife looks like
___23. MAMACITA   W. The big sister, born in Texas
___24. GRANDMOTHER   X. Sits by the window and plays the Spanish radio
___25. RAFAELA   Y. ____ Vargas; has too many children

House on Mango Street Matchig 2 Answer Key

U - 1. PAULINA	A. ____ Garden; kids go there to play
S - 2. VARGAS	B. Dies in hit and run accident
G - 3. ESPERANZA	C. The little sister, born in Chicago
R - 4. BOBO	D. Wants to love and love
I - 5. HEELS	E. Home between Mango and Keeler
L - 6. ZEZE	F. Esperanza wants to eat there
W - 7. LUCY	G. Likes to tell stories
Y - 8. ROSA	H. Type of car Louie's cousin steals
M - 9. EDNA	I. High ____; a woman gives some to the girls to play with
V - 10. EARL	J. Writes poems at night
H - 11. CADILLAC	K. The ____ Boy; sings Pepsi commercials
T - 12. RUTHIE	L. ____ The X; the name Esperanza wants
O - 13. ALICIA	M. Ruthie's mother
N - 14. KEELER	N. Home street between Paulina and Loomis
C - 15. RACHEL	O. Is afraid of mice
F - 16. CANTEEN	P. Likes to drink coconut and papaya juices
E - 17. LOOMIS	Q. Great-____; Esperanza is named for her
D - 18. SALLY	R. Ruthie's dog
J - 19. MINERVA	S. Angel ____ ; tried to fly and dropped from the sky
K - 20. BABY	T. Adult who likes to play
A - 21. MONKEY	U. Home before Keller
B - 22. GERALDO	V. Kids don't agree on what his wife looks like
X - 23. MAMACITA	W. The big sister, born in Texas
Q - 24. GRANDMOTHER	X. Sits by the window and plays the Spanish radio
P - 25. RAFAELA	Y. ____ Vargas; has too many children

Copyrighted

House on Mango Street Matching 3

___ 1. ROSA
___ 2. NENNY
___ 3. MINERVA
___ 4. CATHY
___ 5. RUTHIE
___ 6. ZEZE
___ 7. EDNA
___ 8. BIKE
___ 9. RAFAELA
___ 10. LUCY
___ 11. HEELS
___ 12. MAMACITA
___ 13. RACHEL
___ 14. NACHO
___ 15. DARIUS
___ 16. MUSIC
___ 17. GIL
___ 18. BUICK
___ 19. MONKEY
___ 20. ALICIA
___ 21. LOOMIS
___ 22. GRANDMOTHER
___ 23. PUERTO
___ 24. SIRE
___ 25. MANGO

A. Is afraid of mice
B. ____ The X; the name Esperanza wants
C. Writes poems at night
D. Younger sister to Esperanza
E. ____ Garden; kids go there to play
F. The little sister, born in Chicago
G. Home between Mango and Keeler
H. The big sister, born in Texas
I. Says a cloud was God
J. Esperanza compares her hips to one
K. ____ Rican; Marin's nationality
L. Sits by the window and plays the Spanish radio
M. ____ Box; made Esperanza feel stupid
N. The family owns the house here
O. ____ Vargas; has too many children
P. Owner of the used furniture store
Q. Uncle ____; dances with Esperanza
R. Says the neighborhood is getting bad
S. High ____; a woman gives some to the girls to play with
T. Esperanza noticed him looking at her
U. Adult who likes to play
V. Ruthie's mother
W. Likes to drink coconut and papaya juices
X. Esperanza chipped in to buy it
Y. Great-____; Esperanza is named for her

House on Mango Street Matching 3 Answer Key

O - 1. ROSA	A.	Is afraid of mice
D - 2. NENNY	B.	____ The X; the name Esperanza wants
C - 3. MINERVA	C.	Writes poems at night
R - 4. CATHY	D.	Younger sister to Esperanza
U - 5. RUTHIE	E.	____ Garden; kids go there to play
B - 6. ZEZE	F.	The little sister, born in Chicago
V - 7. EDNA	G.	Home between Mango and Keeler
X - 8. BIKE	H.	The big sister, born in Texas
W - 9. RAFAELA	I.	Says a cloud was God
H - 10. LUCY	J.	Esperanza compares her hips to one
S - 11. HEELS	K.	____ Rican; Marin's nationality
L - 12. MAMACITA	L.	Sits by the window and plays the Spanish radio
F - 13. RACHEL	M.	____ Box; made Esperanza feel stupid
Q - 14. NACHO	N.	The family owns the house here
I - 15. DARIUS	O.	____ Vargas; has too many children
M - 16. MUSIC	P.	Owner of the used furniture store
P - 17. GIL	Q.	Uncle ____; dances with Esperanza
J - 18. BUICK	R.	Says the neighborhood is getting bad
E - 19. MONKEY	S.	High ____; a woman gives some to the girls to play with
A - 20. ALICIA	T.	Esperanza noticed him looking at her
G - 21. LOOMIS	U.	Adult who likes to play
Y - 22. GRANDMOTHER	V.	Ruthie's mother
K - 23. PUERTO	W.	Likes to drink coconut and papaya juices
T - 24. SIRE	X.	Esperanza chipped in to buy it
N - 25. MANGO	Y.	Great-____; Esperanza is named for her

House on Mango Street Matching 4

___ 1. RACHEL   A. Likes to drink coconut and papaya juices
___ 2. LOOMIS   B. Owner of the used furniture store
___ 3. MEXICAN   C. The ____ Boy; sings Pepsi commercials
___ 4. MAMACITA   D. ____-American; Esperanza's nationality
___ 5. PUERTO   E. Three ____ told Esperanza to come back to Mango Street
___ 6. MONKEY   F. Nenny's real name
___ 7. CADILLAC   G. Home between Mango and Keeler
___ 8. HEELS   H. Louie's cousin who sells Avon
___ 9. CORDERO   I. ____ Rican; Marin's nationality
___10. DAVEY   J. Writes poems at night
___11. SIRE   K. Ruthie's mother
___12. BABY   L. Type of car Louie's cousin steals
___13. HORSE   M. High ____; a woman gives some to the girls to play with
___14. BIKE   N. Esperanza chipped in to buy it
___15. MAGDALENA   O. Esperanza noticed him looking at her
___16. EDNA   P. ____ Box; made Esperanza feel stupid
___17. RAFAELA   Q. Dies in hit and run accident
___18. RUTHIE   R. Adult who likes to play
___19. MARIN   S. Sits by the window and plays the Spanish radio
___20. GIL   T. Chinese year of Esperanza's birth
___21. SISTERS   U. ____ Garden; kids go there to play
___22. GERALDO   V. Younger sister to Esperanza
___23. NENNY   W. Esperanza's last name
___24. MINERVA   X. The little sister, born in Chicago
___25. MUSIC   Y. His brother has a crooked eye

House on Mango Street Matching 4 Answer Key

X - 1. RACHEL
G - 2. LOOMIS
D - 3. MEXICAN
S - 4. MAMACITA
I - 5. PUERTO
U - 6. MONKEY
L - 7. CADILLAC
M - 8. HEELS
W - 9. CORDERO
Y - 10. DAVEY
O - 11. SIRE
C - 12. BABY
T - 13. HORSE
N - 14. BIKE
F - 15. MAGDALENA
K - 16. EDNA
A - 17. RAFAELA
R - 18. RUTHIE
H - 19. MARIN
B - 20. GIL
E - 21. SISTERS
Q - 22. GERALDO
V - 23. NENNY
J - 24. MINERVA
P - 25. MUSIC

A. Likes to drink coconut and papaya juices
B. Owner of the used furniture store
C. The ____ Boy; sings Pepsi commercials
D. ____-American; Esperanza's nationality
E. Three ____ told Esperanza to come back to Mango Street
F. Nenny's real name
G. Home between Mango and Keeler
H. Louie's cousin who sells Avon
I. ____ Rican; Marin's nationality
J. Writes poems at night
K. Ruthie's mother
L. Type of car Louie's cousin steals
M. High ____; a woman gives some to the girls to play with
N. Esperanza chipped in to buy it
O. Esperanza noticed him looking at her
P. ____ Box; made Esperanza feel stupid
Q. Dies in hit and run accident
R. Adult who likes to play
S. Sits by the window and plays the Spanish radio
T. Chinese year of Esperanza's birth
U. ____ Garden; kids go there to play
V. Younger sister to Esperanza
W. Esperanza's last name
X. The little sister, born in Chicago
Y. His brother has a crooked eye

House on Mango Street Magic Squares 1

Match the definition with the vocabulary word. Put your answers in the magic squares below. When your answers are correct, all columns and rows will add to the same number.

A. SALLY
B. MAGDALENA
C. ZEZE
D. MAMACITA
E. EDNA
F. GRANDMOTHER
G. ELENITA
H. DARIUS
I. SISTERS
J. LOIS
K. NENNY
L. EARL
M. DAVEY
N. VARGAS
O. ESPERANZA
P. PAULINA

1. Likes to tell stories
2. Sits by the window and plays the Spanish radio
3. Sire's girlfriend
4. Ruthie's mother
5. Three ____ told Esperanza to come back to Mango Street
6. Great-____; Esperanza is named for her
7. Home before Keller
8. ____ The X; the name Esperanza wants
9. Says a cloud was God
10. Younger sister to Esperanza
11. Wants to love and love
12. Angel ____ ; tried to fly and dropped from the sky
13. Nenny's real name
14. His brother has a crooked eye
15. Tells fortunes with cards
16. Kids don't agree on what his wife looks like

A=	B=	C=	D=
E=	F=	G=	H=
I=	J=	K=	L=
M=	N=	O=	P=

House on Mango Street Magic Squares 1 Answer Key

Match the definition with the vocabulary word. Put your answers in the magic squares below. When your answers are correct, all columns and rows will add to the same number.

A. SALLY
B. MAGDALENA
C. ZEZE
D. MAMACITA
E. EDNA
F. GRANDMOTHER
G. ELENITA
H. DARIUS
I. SISTERS
J. LOIS
K. NENNY
L. EARL
M. DAVEY
N. VARGAS
O. ESPERANZA
P. PAULINA

1. Likes to tell stories
2. Sits by the window and plays the Spanish radio
3. Sire's girlfriend
4. Ruthie's mother
5. Three ____ told Esperanza to come back to Mango Street
6. Great-____; Esperanza is named for her
7. Home before Keller
8. ____ The X; the name Esperanza wants
9. Says a cloud was God
10. Younger sister to Esperanza
11. Wants to love and love
12. Angel ____ ; tried to fly and dropped from the sky
13. Nenny's real name
14. His brother has a crooked eye
15. Tells fortunes with cards
16. Kids don't agree on what his wife looks like

A=11	B=13	C=8	D=2
E=4	F=6	G=15	H=9
I=5	J=3	K=10	L=16
M=14	N=12	O=1	P=7

House on Mango Street Magic Squares 2

Match the definition with the vocabulary word. Put your answers in the magic squares below. When your answers are correct, all columns and rows will add to the same number.

A. KEELER
B. MONKEY
C. PUERTO
D. LOOMIS
E. ZEZE
F. MEME
G. ELENITA
H. LUPE
I. LUCY
J. BOBO
K. RACHEL
L. PAULINA
M. GIL
N. MARIN
O. DAVEY
P. HORSE

1. Aunt ____; died the day the girls made fun of her
2. Owner of the used furniture store
3. ____ Garden; kids go there to play
4. The little sister, born in Chicago
5. Ruthie's dog
6. ____ Rican; Marin's nationality
7. Chinese year of Esperanza's birth
8. ____ The X; the name Esperanza wants
9. His brother has a crooked eye
10. Won the contest and broke both arms
11. The big sister, born in Texas
12. Home between Mango and Keeler
13. Home street between Paulina and Loomis
14. Home before Keller
15. Tells fortunes with cards
16. Louie's cousin who sells Avon

A=	B=	C=	D=
E=	F=	G=	H=
I=	J=	K=	L=
M=	N=	O=	P=

House on Mango Street Magic Squares 2 Answer Key

Match the definition with the vocabulary word. Put your answers in the magic squares below. When your answers are correct, all columns and rows will add to the same number.

A. KEELER
B. MONKEY
C. PUERTO
D. LOOMIS
E. ZEZE
F. MEME

G. ELENITA
H. LUPE
I. LUCY
J. BOBO
K. RACHEL
L. PAULINA

M. GIL
N. MARIN
O. DAVEY
P. HORSE

1. Aunt ____; died the day the girls made fun of her
2. Owner of the used furniture store
3. ____ Garden; kids go there to play
4. The little sister, born in Chicago
5. Ruthie's dog
6. ____ Rican; Marin's nationality
7. Chinese year of Esperanza's birth
8. ____ The X; the name Esperanza wants
9. His brother has a crooked eye
10. Won the contest and broke both arms
11. The big sister, born in Texas
12. Home between Mango and Keeler
13. Home street between Paulina and Loomis
14. Home before Keller
15. Tells fortunes with cards
16. Louie's cousin who sells Avon

A=13	B=3	C=6	D=12
E=8	F=10	G=15	H=1
I=11	J=5	K=4	L=14
M=2	N=16	O=9	P=7

House on Mango Street Magic Squares 3

Match the definition with the vocabulary word. Put your answers in the magic squares below. When your answers are correct, all columns and rows will add to the same number.

A. LOIS
B. MEXICAN
C. DAVEY
D. MARIN
E. SISTERS
F. HORSE
G. PUERTO
H. MONKEY
I. KEELER
J. EARL
K. CATHY
L. VARGAS
M. LUCY
N. HEELS
O. GIL
P. GRANDMOTHER

1. Chinese year of Esperanza's birth
2. Home street between Paulina and Loomis
3. Owner of the used furniture store
4. Louie's cousin who sells Avon
5. The big sister, born in Texas
6. ____-American; Esperanza's nationality
7. ____ Garden; kids go there to play
8. Says the neighborhood is getting bad
9. His brother has a crooked eye
10. Great-____; Esperanza is named for her
11. Kids don't agree on what his wife looks like
12. Three ____ told Esperanza to come back to Mango Street
13. Angel ____ ; tried to fly and dropped from the sky
14. ____ Rican; Marin's nationality
15. Sire's girlfriend
16. High ____; a woman gives some to the girls to play with

A=	B=	C=	D=
E=	F=	G=	H=
I=	J=	K=	L=
M=	N=	O=	P=

House on Mango Street Magic Squares 3 Answer Key

Match the definition with the vocabulary word. Put your answers in the magic squares below. When your answers are correct, all columns and rows will add to the same number.

A. LOIS
B. MEXICAN
C. DAVEY
D. MARIN
E. SISTERS
F. HORSE
G. PUERTO
H. MONKEY
I. KEELER
J. EARL
K. CATHY
L. VARGAS
M. LUCY
N. HEELS
O. GIL
P. GRANDMOTHER

1. Chinese year of Esperanza's birth
2. Home street between Paulina and Loomis
3. Owner of the used furniture store
4. Louie's cousin who sells Avon
5. The big sister, born in Texas
6. ____-American; Esperanza's nationality
7. ____ Garden; kids go there to play
8. Says the neighborhood is getting bad
9. His brother has a crooked eye
10. Great-____; Esperanza is named for her
11. Kids don't agree on what his wife looks like
12. Three ____ told Esperanza to come back to Mango Street
13. Angel ____ ; tried to fly and dropped from the sky
14. ____ Rican; Marin's nationality
15. Sire's girlfriend
16. High ____; a woman gives some to the girls to play with

A=15	B=6	C=9	D=4
E=12	F=1	G=14	H=7
I=2	J=11	K=8	L=13
M=5	N=16	O=3	P=10

House on Mango Street Magic Squares 4

Match the definition with the vocabulary word. Put your answers in the magic squares below. When your answers are correct, all columns and rows will add to the same number.

A. MONKEY
B. MEXICAN
C. DARIUS
D. HORSE
E. PAULINA
F. ALICIA
G. PUERTO
H. MANGO
I. NACHO
J. BABY
K. BIKE
L. MAMACITA
M. TREES
N. MAGDALENA
O. HEELS
P. CORDERO

1. ____ Garden; kids go there to play
2. Nenny's real name
3. The ____ Boy; sings Pepsi commercials
4. Home before Keller
5. ____ Rican; Marin's nationality
6. Sits by the window and plays the Spanish radio
7. Esperanza's last name
8. Says a cloud was God
9. High ____; a woman gives some to the girls to play with
10. Chinese year of Esperanza's birth
11. The family owns the house here
12. Esperanza chipped in to buy it
13. Uncle ____; dances with Esperanza
14. Is afraid of mice
15. ____-American; Esperanza's nationality
16. The only ones who understand Esperanza

A=	B=	C=	D=
E=	F=	G=	H=
I=	J=	K=	L=
M=	N=	O=	P=

House on Mango Street Magic Squares 4 Answer Key

Match the definition with the vocabulary word. Put your answers in the magic squares below. When your answers are correct, all columns and rows will add to the same number.

A. MONKEY
B. MEXICAN
C. DARIUS
D. HORSE
E. PAULINA
F. ALICIA
G. PUERTO
H. MANGO
I. NACHO
J. BABY
K. BIKE
L. MAMACITA
M. TREES
N. MAGDALENA
O. HEELS
P. CORDERO

1. ____ Garden; kids go there to play
2. Nenny's real name
3. The ____ Boy; sings Pepsi commercials
4. Home before Keller
5. ____ Rican; Marin's nationality
6. Sits by the window and plays the Spanish radio
7. Esperanza's last name
8. Says a cloud was God
9. High ____; a woman gives some to the girls to play with
10. Chinese year of Esperanza's birth
11. The family owns the house here
12. Esperanza chipped in to buy it
13. Uncle ____; dances with Esperanza
14. Is afraid of mice
15. ____-American; Esperanza's nationality
16. The only ones who understand Esperanza

A=1	B=15	C=8	D=10
E=4	F=14	G=5	H=11
I=13	J=3	K=12	L=6
M=16	N=2	O=9	P=7

House on Mango Street Word Search 1

```
T R E E S D K M S I S T E R S S B P
M U S I C A E N A M L N C G B I R S
A T I N E L E J M G E R A L D O Y W
M L X A Z E L D I H D Z D C S L B P
D V R B T A E Z N Z N A I A H H M O
B L V N P F R H E A B C L C V O E N
W U A D M A X E R V X A L E L N M F
S C I M O R U E V Y V T A S N L E K
B A N C N M P L A B A H C R O A Y M
N A L Y K S E S I I R Y N O R N A Z
E W B L E S X X C N G N M H N N C S
N S D Y Y L I I I N A I D E G E U T
N T A V U Y L R I C S K B O K I Z P
Y X V P R A G R E K A Q R I R Y L V
P U E R T O A Z E Z E N B A L U C Y
H J Y X K M B H H C O R D E R O P M
```

Angel ____ ; tried to fly and dropped from the sky (6)
Aunt ____; died the day the girls made fun of her (4)
Chinese year of Esperanza's birth (5)
Dies in hit and run accident (7)
Esperanza chipped in to buy it (4)
Esperanza compares her hips to one (5)
Esperanza noticed him looking at her (4)
Esperanza wants to eat there (7)
Esperanza's last name (7)
High ____; a woman gives some to the girls to play with (5)
His brother has a crooked eye (5)
Home before Keller (7)
Home between Mango and Keeler (6)
Home street between Paulina and Loomis (6)
Is afraid of mice (6)
Kids don't agree on what his wife looks like (4)
Likes to drink coconut and papaya juices (7)
Likes to tell stories (9)
Louie's cousin who sells Avon (5)
Mr. ____; grocery store owner (5)
Nenny's real name (9)
Owner of the used furniture store (3)

Ruthie's dog (4)
Ruthie's mother (4)
Says a cloud was God (6)
Says the neighborhood is getting bad (5)
Sire's girlfriend (4)
Tells fortunes with cards (7)
The ____ Boy; sings Pepsi commercials (4)
The big sister, born in Texas (4)
The family owns the house here (5)
The only ones who understand Esperanza (5)
Three ____ told Esperanza to come back to Mango Street (7)
Type of car Louie's cousin steals (8)
Uncle ____; dances with Esperanza (5)
Wants to love and love (5)
Won the contest and broke both arms (4)
Writes poems at night (7)
Younger sister to Esperanza (5)
____ Box; made Esperanza feel stupid (5)
____ Garden; kids go there to play (6)
____ Rican; Marin's nationality (6)
____ The X; the name Esperanza wants (4)
____ Vargas; has too many children (4)
____-American; Esperanza's nationality (7)

House on Mango Street Word Search 1 Answer Key

```
T R E E S     K M S I S T E R S S
M U S I C A E N A     N C   B   R
A T I N E L E   M G E R A L D O
        A   E L D I   D Z D C S L B
      R   T A E N   N A I A H   M O
B L   N P F R H E A   C L E     O E
  U A   I O M A E R   A L       M
S C     O R U E V   V T A S N L E
B A     C N M P L A   A H C R O A Y M
N L     K S E S I R   R Y O N A
E   B L E S X C N G     M H N N   S
N   D Y Y L I I N A     I E G E U
N   A   U L R I C S   B   O K I
Y   V P   A   R E   A     I R   L
P U E R T O A Z E Z E N B A L U C Y
      Y     M         C O R D E R O
```

Angel ____; tried to fly and dropped from the sky (6)
Aunt ____; died the day the girls made fun of her (4)
Chinese year of Esperanza's birth (5)
Dies in hit and run accident (7)
Esperanza chipped in to buy it (4)
Esperanza compares her hips to one (5)
Esperanza noticed him looking at her (4)
Esperanza wants to eat there (7)
Esperanza's last name (7)
High ____; a woman gives some to the girls to play with (5)
His brother has a crooked eye (5)
Home before Keller (7)
Home between Mango and Keeler (6)
Home street between Paulina and Loomis (6)
Is afraid of mice (6)
Kids don't agree on what his wife looks like (4)
Likes to drink coconut and papaya juices (7)
Likes to tell stories (9)
Louie's cousin who sells Avon (5)
Mr. ____; grocery store owner (5)
Nenny's real name (9)
Owner of the used furniture store (3)

Ruthie's dog (4)
Ruthie's mother (4)
Says a cloud was God (6)
Says the neighborhood is getting bad (5)
Sire's girlfriend (4)
Tells fortunes with cards (7)
The ____ Boy; sings Pepsi commercials (4)
The big sister, born in Texas (4)
The family owns the house here (5)
The only ones who understand Esperanza (5)
Three ____ told Esperanza to come back to Mango Street (7)
Type of car Louie's cousin steals (8)
Uncle ____; dances with Esperanza (5)
Wants to love and love (5)
Won the contest and broke both arms (4)
Writes poems at night (7)
Younger sister to Esperanza (5)
____ Box; made Esperanza feel stupid (5)
____ Garden; kids go there to play (6)
____ Rican; Marin's nationality (6)
____ The X; the name Esperanza wants (4)
____ Vargas; has too many children (4)
____-American; Esperanza's nationality (7)

House on Mango Street Word Search 2

```
D A V E Y E K N O M H L M B O B O D
A S W J Z X A P K A E O I N B N P S
N A R P G C M Q X N E O N E E C B W
E L U Y H T A C G G L M E N N N W G
L L T O P U E R T O S I R N N P J Q
A Y H P F T D A R I U S V Y Y T C G
D F I O E H S F F Z A N A N T R I J
G T E C R A Q A B N A P A O M E S K
A E N J B S R E I U T C G R A E U F
M B R A C H E L S S I S T E R S M Q
B V B A V L U A I X N C P D I O K E
B Y L V L A Q O E Z E U K R N H S K
C I N V P D L M T E L Q E O G I L A
G Y K B N S O S D Z E M J C H X U M
R E L E E K N N M E A L I C I A C Y
V A R G A S A C A D I L L A C T Y X
```

Adult who likes to play (6)
Angel ____ ; tried to fly and dropped from the sky (6)
Aunt ____ ; died the day the girls made fun of her (4)
Chinese year of Esperanza's birth (5)
Dies in hit and run accident (7)
Esperanza chipped in to buy it (4)
Esperanza compares her hips to one (5)
Esperanza noticed him looking at her (4)
Esperanza's last name (7)
High ____ ; a woman gives some to the girls to play with (5)
His brother has a crooked eye (5)
Home before Keller (7)
Home between Mango and Keeler (6)
Home street between Paulina and Loomis (6)
Is afraid of mice (6)
Kids don't agree on what his wife looks like (4)
Likes to drink coconut and papaya juices (7)
Louie's cousin who sells Avon (5)
Mr. ____ ; grocery store owner (5)
Nenny's real name (9)
Owner of the used furniture store (3)
Ruthie's dog (4)

Ruthie's mother (4)
Says a cloud was God (6)
Says the neighborhood is getting bad (5)
Sire's girlfriend (4)
Tells fortunes with cards (7)
The ____ Boy; sings Pepsi commercials (4)
The big sister, born in Texas (4)
The family owns the house here (5)
The little sister, born in Chicago (6)
The only ones who understand Esperanza (5)
Three ____ told Esperanza to come back to Mango Street (7)
Type of car Louie's cousin steals (8)
Uncle ____ ; dances with Esperanza (5)
Wants to love and love (5)
Won the contest and broke both arms (4)
Writes poems at night (7)
Younger sister to Esperanza (5)
____ Box; made Esperanza feel stupid (5)
____ Garden; kids go there to play (6)
____ Rican; Marin's nationality (6)
____ The X; the name Esperanza wants (4)
____ Vargas; has too many children (4)
____-American; Esperanza's nationality (7)

House on Mango Street Word Search 2 Answer Key

```
D A V E Y E K N O M H L M B O B O
  A S           A       A E O I N B
N A R           C       N E O N E E
E L U Y H T A C         G L M E N N
L L T O P U E R T O S I R N N
A Y H       D A R I U S V Y   T C
D   I O E       F   A   A N   R I
G   E   R A   A B N A   O M E S
A E     B S R E I U T   C R A E U
M   R A C H E L   S I S T E R S M
    B A   U A I X N C P D I O   E
B Y     L A   O E Z E U K R N   S
    I     P D L M E L   E O G I L A
      K       O   D Z E     C   U
R E L E E K   N   E A L I C I A C
V A R G A S A C A D I L L A C   Y
```

Adult who likes to play (6)
Angel ____ ; tried to fly and dropped from the sky (6)
Aunt ____; died the day the girls made fun of her (4)
Chinese year of Esperanza's birth (5)
Dies in hit and run accident (7)
Esperanza chipped in to buy it (4)
Esperanza compares her hips to one (5)
Esperanza noticed him looking at her (4)
Esperanza's last name (7)
High ____; a woman gives some to the girls to play with (5)
His brother has a crooked eye (5)
Home before Keller (7)
Home between Mango and Keeler (6)
Home street between Paulina and Loomis (6)
Is afraid of mice (6)
Kids don't agree on what his wife looks like (4)
Likes to drink coconut and papaya juices (7)
Louie's cousin who sells Avon (5)
Mr. ____; grocery store owner (5)
Nenny's real name (9)
Owner of the used furniture store (3)
Ruthie's dog (4)

Ruthie's mother (4)
Says a cloud was God (6)
Says the neighborhood is getting bad (5)
Sire's girlfriend (4)
Tells fortunes with cards (7)
The ____ Boy; sings Pepsi commercials (4)
The big sister, born in Texas (4)
The family owns the house here (5)
The little sister, born in Chicago (6)
The only ones who understand Esperanza (5)
Three ____ told Esperanza to come back to Mango Street (7)
Type of car Louie's cousin steals (8)
Uncle ____; dances with Esperanza (5)
Wants to love and love (5)
Won the contest and broke both arms (4)
Writes poems at night (7)
Younger sister to Esperanza (5)
____ Box; made Esperanza feel stupid (5)
____ Garden; kids go there to play (6)
____ Rican; Marin's nationality (6)
____ The X; the name Esperanza wants (4)
____ Vargas; has too many children (4)
____-American; Esperanza's nationality (7)

House on Mango Street Word Search 3

```
L C H G B M K L K C H D Z X V R M X D M N S B T S
O B O B L U P E A N D E Y R A C H E L R A E G I L
T A R R N Q I N Y V Z E E E A R R C A G C N O I D
R L S J D P T C Z E V H V L L I X F R B H L G Z L
E I E Y L E J B K A T M L E S M A A D H O C B O Y
U C G Z E K R L D O Y I M E M E V P A U L I N A D
P I E N W I R O M N D N Y K L X Q T R K F S F D D
R A R P C B D D N A M E P A J I I T I S G U S T X
O M A C X W N E C Q X R K H M C K N U M T M D F L
S Q L N A A B P T L W V Q R A A X L S R U T H I E
A R D J R T N L R C U A H M R N G R M O N K E Y Z
K L O G E B H Q E T C C A Z I Y E D N H M P G N V
C D O S A L L Y E W J M Y Z N T Q C A E P X H R S
S P V O G H E J S F G J K T S K B G X L N C Z Z K
K Y C Y M P Q N M L Y K W I J F K J T V E N R R C
C Z B G T I J L I Y R H S C C C V L J T L N Y H D
Y A D B Z H S R K T E S P E R A N Z A D P G A T Q
B Q D L M T H P L N A R Z C S D L T S V L W Q S Z
W R W G K K G Y C J C J X V L Y C F Z T S C Y G X
C F B V G R P R H K W W Q N W D N T M J Q J M L G
```

ALICIA	GIL	MUSIC
BABY	GRANDMOTHER	NACHO
BENNY	HEELS	NENNY
BIKE	HORSE	PAULINA
BOBO	KEELER	PUERTO
BUICK	LOIS	RACHEL
CADILLAC	LOOMIS	RAFAELA
CANTEEN	LUCY	ROSA
CATHY	LUPE	RUTHIE
CORDERO	MAGDALENA	SALLY
DARIUS	MAMACITA	SIRE
DAVEY	MANGO	SISTERS
EARL	MARIN	TREES
EDNA	MEME	VARGAS
ELENITA	MEXICAN	ZEZE
ESPERANZA	MINERVA	
GERALDO	MONKEY	

House on Mango Street Word Search 3 Answer Key

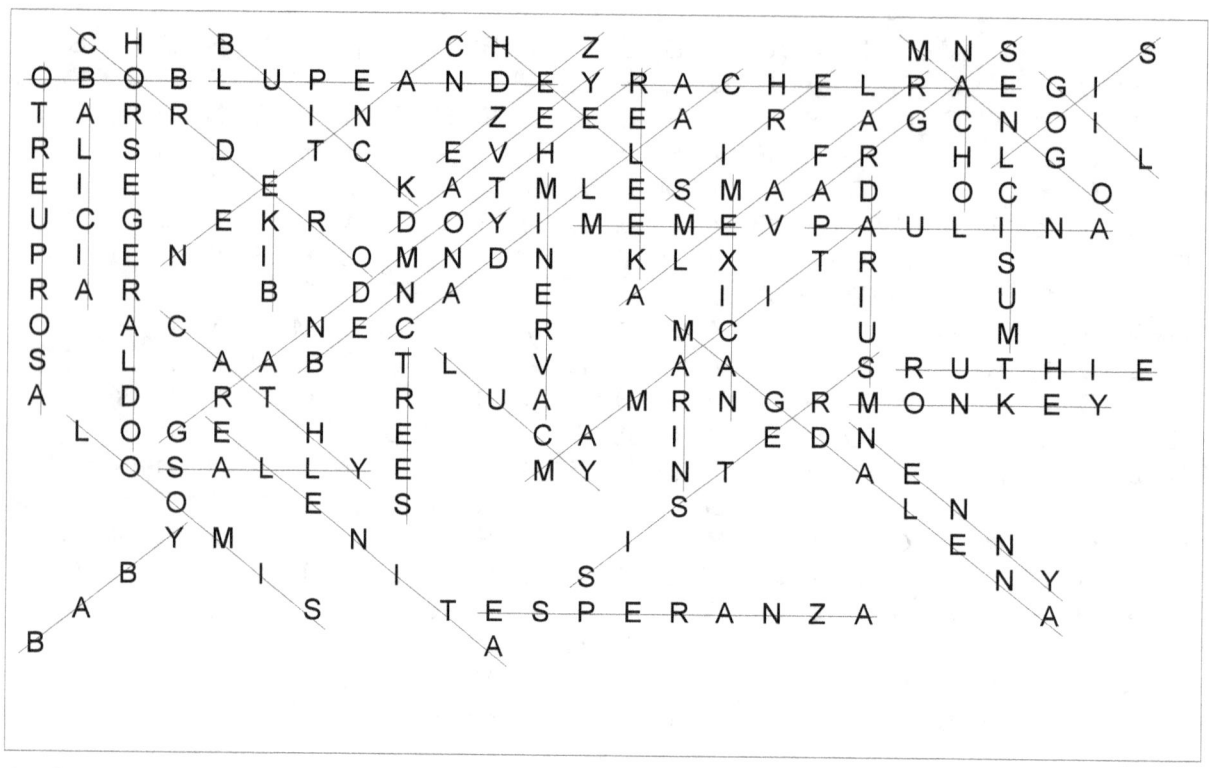

ALICIA	GIL	MUSIC
BABY	GRANDMOTHER	NACHO
BENNY	HEELS	NENNY
BIKE	HORSE	PAULINA
BOBO	KEELER	PUERTO
BUICK	LOIS	RACHEL
CADILLAC	LOOMIS	RAFAELA
CANTEEN	LUCY	ROSA
CATHY	LUPE	RUTHIE
CORDERO	MAGDALENA	SALLY
DARIUS	MAMACITA	SIRE
DAVEY	MANGO	SISTERS
EARL	MARIN	TREES
EDNA	MEME	VARGAS
ELENITA	MEXICAN	ZEZE
ESPERANZA	MINERVA	
GERALDO	MONKEY	

House on Mango Street Word Search 4

```
M I N E R V A P N M A M W P S V E P S A L L Y N J
U E Z V K V Y W U I H R O I M P A S A G L H Y B Y
S G X L B G K J C E S Q M N V W P R P U M J C O R
I E Z I P T O I Q L R O T B K M X C G E L K V B G
C R R L C R L R Z D O T S W M E P A M A R I S O V
P A B V E A M B Y L M K O G A D Y D C H S A N R N
T L P D H K N M P X B Q V H G F F I X Q R H N A Z
C D R Y W W K T R M L G W B D N H L Z H S T T Z P
R O T Q Z D L X Z D Z R M Z A Y T L H Q J K F B A
C H M H J N N S V R X A D Y L J Q A P P C Q W B X
P T N F R B W N A D D N F S E Z H C R K X T L N C
X R T C K L B C E X N D M F N Y T S H L B Q P E Y
C E X Q E H H P R J R M N A A E P C H Q H A N N G
Y E Y E E E Y M I O T O Y H M V C G L X H E B N D
D S I O L U P E S I S T E R S A L E A F A R E Y S
N R T C E E W A Z K U H Z B T D C B G O R S C L Z
L A N Q R D N L C L I E Z H B Z I I G V R U W N S
L C C W M L N I R V R R Y V W K E N T O L X X L S
R U T H I E U A T C A N T E E N A Z H A M E M E L
G I L Z O B E Y H A D N I R A M R B E N N Y H Q M
```

ALICIA	GIL	MUSIC
BABY	GRANDMOTHER	NACHO
BENNY	HEELS	NENNY
BIKE	HORSE	PAULINA
BOBO	KEELER	PUERTO
BUICK	LOIS	RACHEL
CADILLAC	LOOMIS	RAFAELA
CANTEEN	LUCY	ROSA
CATHY	LUPE	RUTHIE
CORDERO	MAGDALENA	SALLY
DARIUS	MAMACITA	SIRE
DAVEY	MANGO	SISTERS
EARL	MARIN	TREES
EDNA	MEME	VARGAS
ELENITA	MEXICAN	ZEZE
ESPERANZA	MINERVA	
GERALDO	MONKEY	

House on Mango Street Word Search 4 Answer Key

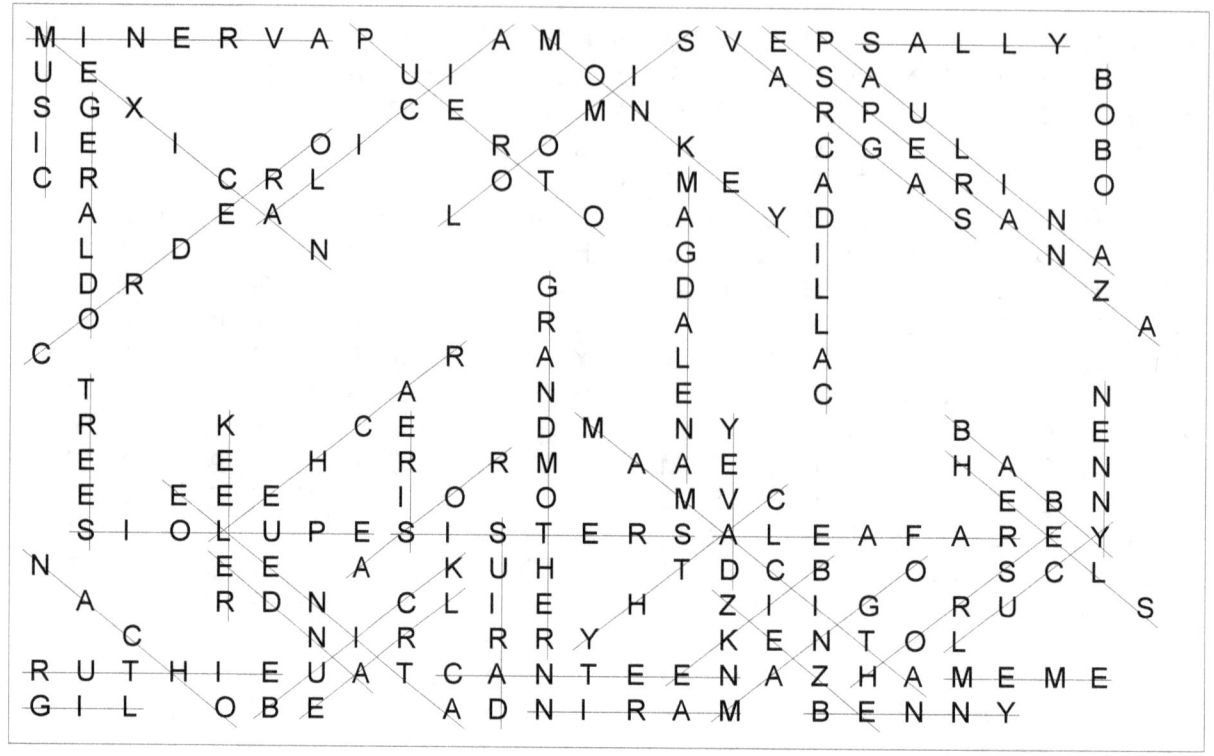

ALICIA	GIL	MUSIC
BABY	GRANDMOTHER	NACHO
BENNY	HEELS	NENNY
BIKE	HORSE	PAULINA
BOBO	KEELER	PUERTO
BUICK	LOIS	RACHEL
CADILLAC	LOOMIS	RAFAELA
CANTEEN	LUCY	ROSA
CATHY	LUPE	RUTHIE
CORDERO	MAGDALENA	SALLY
DARIUS	MAMACITA	SIRE
DAVEY	MANGO	SISTERS
EARL	MARIN	TREES
EDNA	MEME	VARGAS
ELENITA	MEXICAN	ZEZE
ESPERANZA	MINERVA	
GERALDO	MONKEY	

House on Mango Street Crossword 1

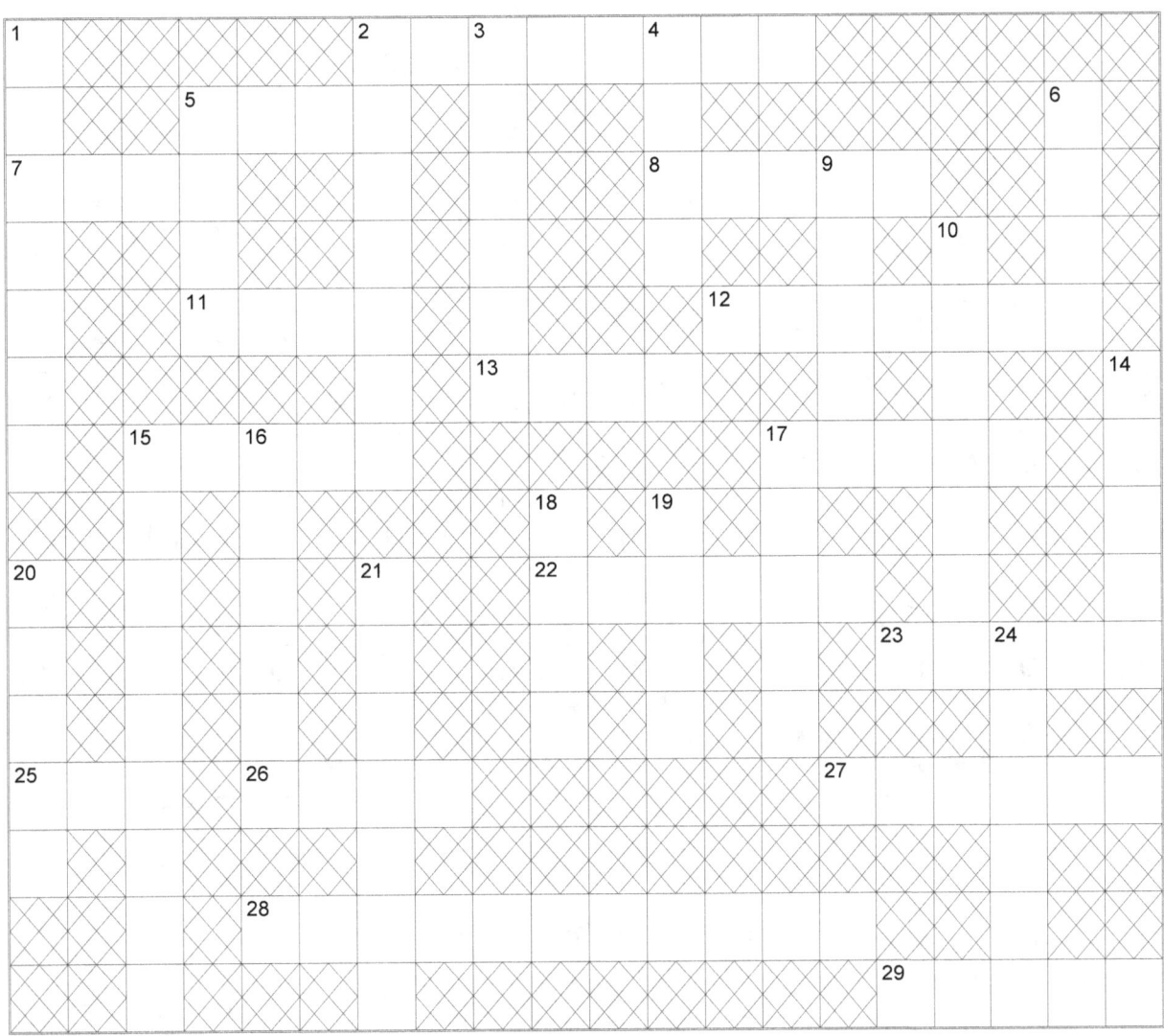

Across
2. Type of car Louie's cousin steals
5. Ruthie's mother
7. ____ Vargas; has too many children
8. Says the neighborhood is getting bad
11. Aunt ____; died the day the girls made fun of her
12. Dies in hit and run accident
13. Esperanza noticed him looking at her
15. Louie's cousin who sells Avon
17. Mr. ____; grocery store owner
22. Is afraid of mice
23. His brother has a crooked eye
25. Owner of the used furniture store
26. Sire's girlfriend
27. ____ Rican; Marin's nationality
28. Great-____; Esperanza is named for her
29. ____ Box; made Esperanza feel stupid

Down
1. Esperanza's last name
2. Esperanza wants to eat there
3. Says a cloud was God
4. The big sister, born in Texas
5. Kids don't agree on what his wife looks like
6. Ruthie's dog
9. Chinese year of Esperanza's birth
10. Tells fortunes with cards
14. Younger sister to Esperanza
15. Nenny's real name
16. The little sister, born in Chicago
17. Esperanza compares her hips to one
18. The ____ Boy; sings Pepsi commercials
19. Esperanza chipped in to buy it
20. The family owns the house here
21. ____-American; Esperanza's nationality
24. Angel ____ ; tried to fly and dropped from the sky

House on Mango Street Crossword 1 Answer Key

Across
2. Type of car Louie's cousin steals
5. Ruthie's mother
7. ____ Vargas; has too many children
8. Says the neighborhood is getting bad
11. Aunt ____; died the day the girls made fun of her
12. Dies in hit and run accident
13. Esperanza noticed him looking at her
15. Louie's cousin who sells Avon
17. Mr. ____; grocery store owner
22. Is afraid of mice
23. His brother has a crooked eye
25. Owner of the used furniture store
26. Sire's girlfriend
27. ____ Rican; Marin's nationality
28. Great-____; Esperanza is named for her
29. ____ Box; made Esperanza feel stupid

Down
1. Esperanza's last name
2. Esperanza wants to eat there
3. Says a cloud was God
4. The big sister, born in Texas
5. Kids don't agree on what his wife looks like
6. Ruthie's dog
9. Chinese year of Esperanza's birth
10. Tells fortunes with cards
14. Younger sister to Esperanza
15. Nenny's real name
16. The little sister, born in Chicago
17. Esperanza compares her hips to one
18. The ____ Boy; sings Pepsi commercials
19. Esperanza chipped in to buy it
20. The family owns the house here
21. ____-American; Esperanza's nationality
24. Angel ____; tried to fly and dropped from the sky

House on Mango Street Crossword 2

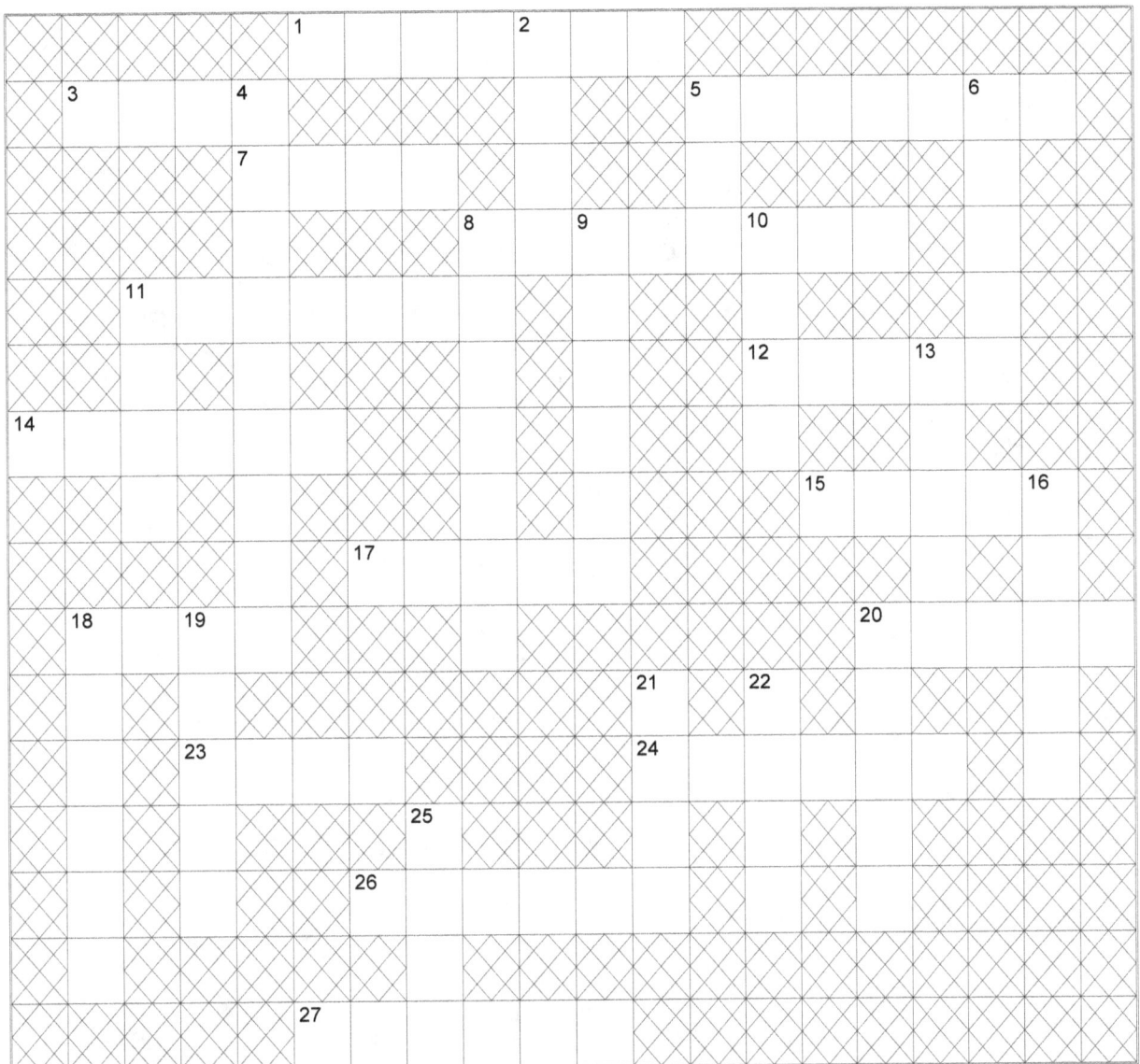

Across
1. Esperanza's last name
3. Aunt ____; died the day the girls made fun of her
5. Dies in hit and run accident
7. Esperanza noticed him looking at her
8. Type of car Louie's cousin steals
11. Tells fortunes with cards
12. Says the neighborhood is getting bad
14. Angel ____ ; tried to fly and dropped from the sky
15. Louie's cousin who sells Avon
17. High ____; a woman gives some to the girls to play with
18. ____ Vargas; has too many children
20. Mr. ____; grocery store owner
23. Sire's girlfriend
24. Is afraid of mice
26. ____ Garden; kids go there to play
27. Home between Mango and Keeler

Down
2. Ruthie's mother
4. Likes to tell stories
5. Owner of the used furniture store
6. His brother has a crooked eye
8. Esperanza wants to eat there
9. Says a cloud was God
10. The big sister, born in Texas
11. Kids don't agree on what his wife looks like
13. Chinese year of Esperanza's birth
16. Younger sister to Esperanza
18. The little sister, born in Chicago
19. Wants to love and love
20. Esperanza compares her hips to one
21. The ____ Boy; sings Pepsi commercials
22. Esperanza chipped in to buy it
25. Ruthie's dog

House on Mango Street Crossword 2 Answer Key

					¹C	O	R	²D	E	R	O				
	³L	U	⁴P	E				D			⁵G	E	R	A	⁶L	D	O
			⁷S	I	R	E		N			I				A
			P				⁸C	A	⁹D	I	¹⁰L	L	A	C	V
		¹¹E	L	E	N	I	T	A		A		U			E
			A		R		N		R		¹²C	A	¹³T	H	Y
¹⁴V	A	R	G	A	S		T		I		Y		O		
			L		N		E		U			¹⁵M	A	R	¹⁶N
			Z		¹⁷H	E	E	L	S			S			E
¹⁸R	¹⁹O	S	A				N				²⁰B	E	N	N	Y
	A		A						²¹B		²²B	U			N
C	²³L	O	I	S				²⁴A	L	I	C	I	A		Y
H	L				²⁵B			B			K		C		
E	Y			²⁶M	O	N	K	E	Y		E		K		
L					B										
			²⁷L	O	O	M	I	S							

Across
1. Esperanza's last name
3. Aunt ____; died the day the girls made fun of her
5. Dies in hit and run accident
7. Esperanza noticed him looking at her
8. Type of car Louie's cousin steals
11. Tells fortunes with cards
12. Says the neighborhood is getting bad
14. Angel ____ ; tried to fly and dropped from the sky
15. Louie's cousin who sells Avon
17. High ____; a woman gives some to the girls to play with
18. ____ Vargas; has too many children
20. Mr. ____; grocery store owner
23. Sire's girlfriend
24. Is afraid of mice
26. ____ Garden; kids go there to play
27. Home between Mango and Keeler

Down
2. Ruthie's mother
4. Likes to tell stories
5. Owner of the used furniture store
6. His brother has a crooked eye
8. Esperanza wants to eat there
9. Says a cloud was God
10. The big sister, born in Texas
11. Kids don't agree on what his wife looks like
13. Chinese year of Esperanza's birth
16. Younger sister to Esperanza
18. The little sister, born in Chicago
19. Wants to love and love
20. Esperanza compares her hips to one
21. The ____ Boy; sings Pepsi commercials
22. Esperanza chipped in to buy it
25. Ruthie's dog

House on Mango Street Crossword 3

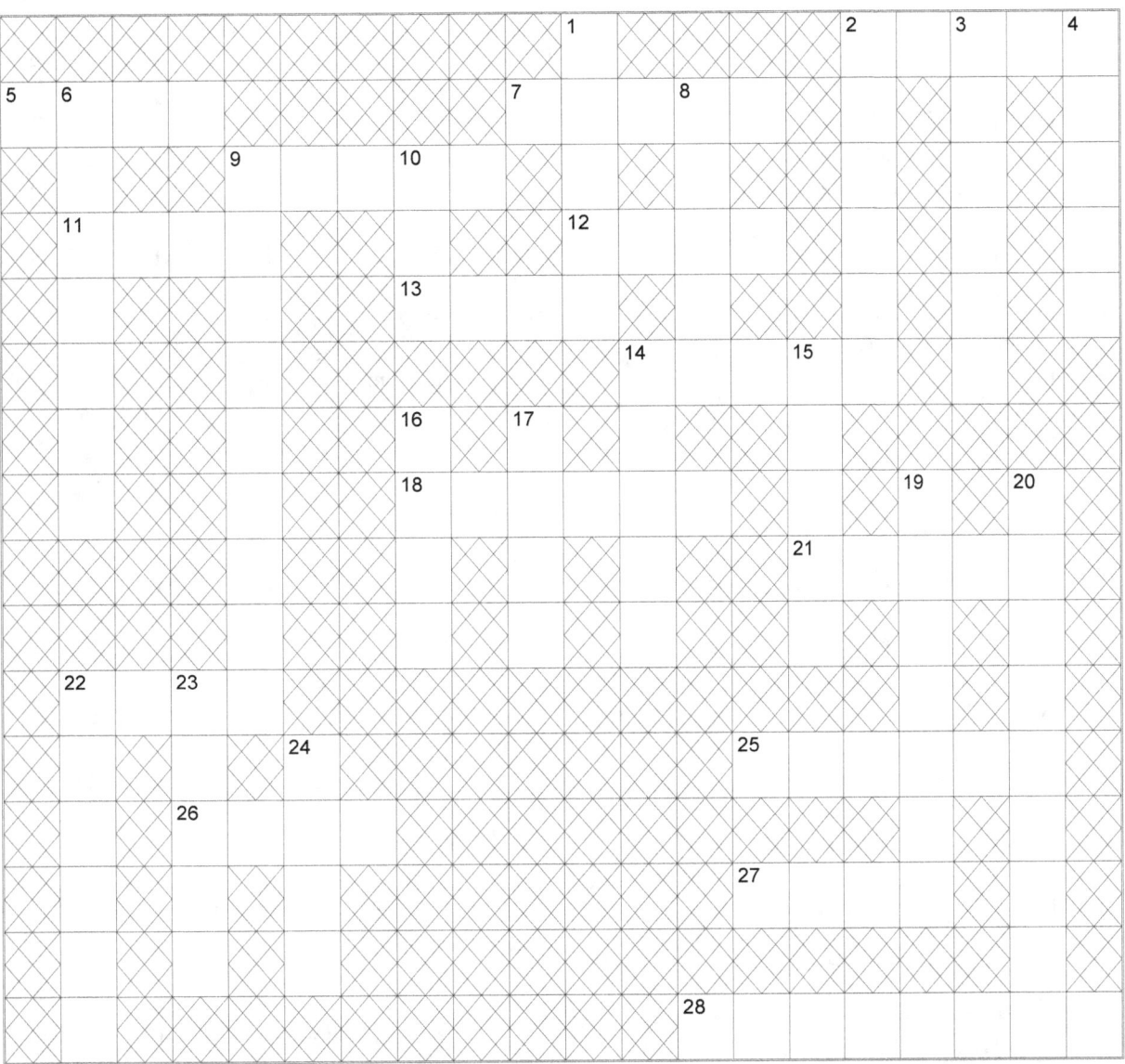

Across
2. Louie's cousin who sells Avon
5. Won the contest and broke both arms
7. Says the neighborhood is getting bad
9. The family owns the house here
11. Ruthie's mother
12. Kids don't agree on what his wife looks like
13. The big sister, born in Texas
14. Mr. ____; grocery store owner
18. Is afraid of mice
21. High ____; a woman gives some to the girls to play with
22. ____ Vargas; has too many children
25. Home street between Paulina and Loomis
26. Sire's girlfriend
27. Ruthie's dog
28. Type of car Louie's cousin steals

Down
1. His brother has a crooked eye
2. ____ Garden; kids go there to play
3. The little sister, born in Chicago
4. Younger sister to Esperanza
6. Tells fortunes with cards
8. Chinese year of Esperanza's birth
9. Nenny's real name
10. Owner of the used furniture store
14. Esperanza compares her hips to one
15. Uncle ____; dances with Esperanza
16. The ____ Boy; sings Pepsi commercials
17. Esperanza chipped in to buy it
19. Dies in hit and run accident
20. Likes to tell stories
22. Adult who likes to play
23. Wants to love and love
24. Esperanza noticed him looking at her

House on Mango Street Crossword 3 Answer Key

							1 D		2 M	3 A	4 N
5 M	6 E	M	E			7 C	A	8 T H Y	O	A	E
	L		9 M	A	10 N G O		V	O	N	C	N
	11 E D N A				I		12 E A R L		K	H	N
	N		G		13 L U C Y		S		E	E	Y
	I		D				14 B	E 15 N	N Y	L	
	T		A		16 B	17 B	U		A		
	A		L		18 A L I C I A			C	19 G	20 E	
			E		B	K	C		21 H E E L S		
			N		Y	E	K		O	R	P
	22 R	23 O S A							A	E	
	U	A	24 S				25 K E E L E R		
	T	26 L O I S					D	A	
	H	L	R				27 B O B O	N	
	I	Y	E					Z	
	E						28 C A D I L L A C

Across
2. Louie's cousin who sells Avon
5. Won the contest and broke both arms
7. Says the neighborhood is getting bad
9. The family owns the house here
11. Ruthie's mother
12. Kids don't agree on what his wife looks like
13. The big sister, born in Texas
14. Mr. ____; grocery store owner
18. Is afraid of mice
21. High ____; a woman gives some to the girls to play with
22. ____ Vargas; has too many children
25. Home street between Paulina and Loomis
26. Sire's girlfriend
27. Ruthie's dog
28. Type of car Louie's cousin steals

Down
1. His brother has a crooked eye
2. ____ Garden; kids go there to play
3. The little sister, born in Chicago
4. Younger sister to Esperanza
6. Tells fortunes with cards
8. Chinese year of Esperanza's birth
9. Nenny's real name
10. Owner of the used furniture store
14. Esperanza compares her hips to one
15. Uncle ____; dances with Esperanza
16. The ____ Boy; sings Pepsi commercials
17. Esperanza chipped in to buy it
19. Dies in hit and run accident
20. Likes to tell stories
22. Adult who likes to play
23. Wants to love and love
24. Esperanza noticed him looking at her

House on Mango Street Crossword 4

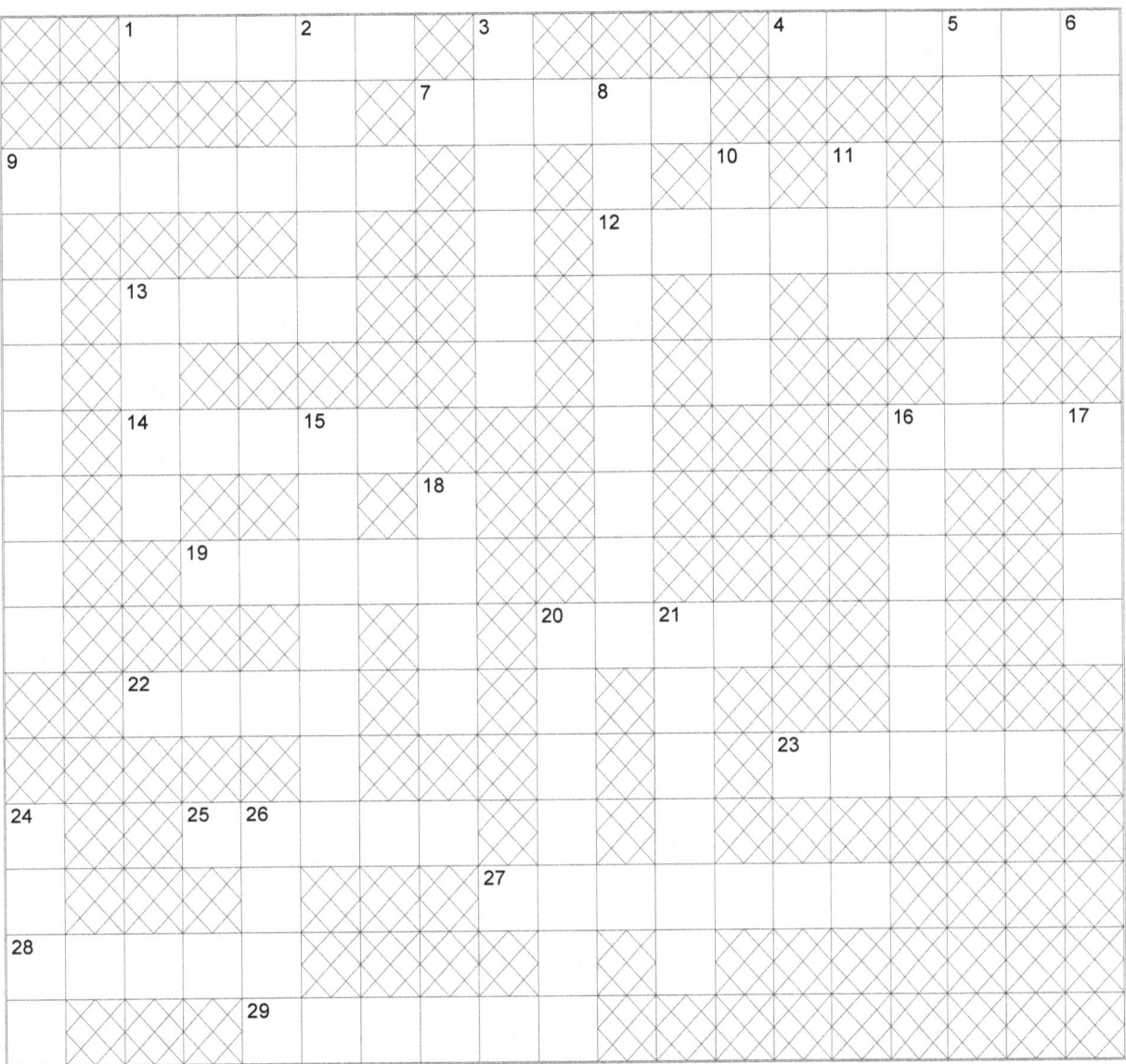

Across
1. Says the neighborhood is getting bad
4. Angel ____ ; tried to fly and dropped from the sky
7. His brother has a crooked eye
9. Esperanza's last name
12. Home before Keller
13. Esperanza chipped in to buy it
14. Esperanza compares her hips to one
16. Sire's girlfriend
19. The family owns the house here
20. Kids don't agree on what his wife looks like
22. Aunt ____; died the day the girls made fun of her
23. ____ Box; made Esperanza feel stupid
25. Mr. ____; grocery store owner
27. Writes poems at night
28. Louie's cousin who sells Avon
29. Is afraid of mice

Down
2. Chinese year of Esperanza's birth
3. Says a cloud was God
5. Dies in hit and run accident
6. Wants to love and love
8. Likes to tell stories
9. Type of car Louie's cousin steals
10. The big sister, born in Texas
11. Owner of the used furniture store
13. The ____ Boy; sings Pepsi commercials
15. Esperanza wants to eat there
16. Home between Mango and Keeler
17. Esperanza noticed him looking at her
18. Ruthie's dog
20. Tells fortunes with cards
21. The little sister, born in Chicago
24. Won the contest and broke both arms
26. Ruthie's mother

House on Mango Street Crossword 4 Answer Key

	1 C	A	2 T	H	Y	3 D			4 V	A	5 R	G	A	6 S
			O		7 D	A	V	8 E	Y			E		A
9 C	O	R	D	E	R	O		S		10 L	11 G	R		L
A			S			I		12 P	A	U	L	I	N	A
D		13 B	I	K	E			U		E		C		L
I		A						S		R		Y		L
L		14 B	U	15 C	K			R		A			16 L	17 S
L		Y		A		18 B		A		N			O	I
A		19 M	A	N	G	O		Z					O	R
C				T		B		20 E	A	21 R	L			E
		22 L	U	P	E					A		23 M	U	S	I	C
24 M		25 B	26 E	N	N	Y		N		C		I		
E			D				27 M	I	N	E	R	V	A	
28 M	A	R	I	N				T		L				
E		29 A	L	I	C	I	A							

Across
1. Says the neighborhood is getting bad
4. Angel ____ ; tried to fly and dropped from the sky
7. His brother has a crooked eye
9. Esperanza's last name
12. Home before Keller
13. Esperanza chipped in to buy it
14. Esperanza compares her hips to one
16. Sire's girlfriend
19. The family owns the house here
20. Kids don't agree on what his wife looks like
22. Aunt ____; died the day the girls made fun of her
23. ____ Box; made Esperanza feel stupid
25. Mr. ____; grocery store owner
27. Writes poems at night
28. Louie's cousin who sells Avon
29. Is afraid of mice

Down
2. Chinese year of Esperanza's birth
3. Says a cloud was God
5. Dies in hit and run accident
6. Wants to love and love
8. Likes to tell stories
9. Type of car Louie's cousin steals
10. The big sister, born in Texas
11. Owner of the used furniture store
13. The ____ Boy; sings Pepsi commercials
15. Esperanza wants to eat there
16. Home between Mango and Keeler
17. Esperanza noticed him looking at her
18. Ruthie's dog
20. Tells fortunes with cards
21. The little sister, born in Chicago
24. Won the contest and broke both arms
26. Ruthie's mother

44
Copyrighted

House on Mango Street

ESPERANZA	MAGDALENA	VARGAS	LUCY	SISTERS
MANGO	EDNA	TREES	MINERVA	NENNY
ROSA	MARIN	FREE SPACE	DARIUS	NACHO
LOOMIS	MAMACITA	LUPE	BIKE	GERALDO
BUICK	EARL	MEME	ALICIA	CORDERO

House on Mango Street

MUSIC	DAVEY	SALLY	SIRE	RUTHIE
BOBO	MEXICAN	MONKEY	HEELS	ELENITA
HORSE	LOIS	FREE SPACE	CATHY	GIL
PUERTO	RACHEL	PAULINA	RAFAELA	CANTEEN
GRANDMOTHER	BABY	BENNY	KEELER	CORDERO

House on Mango Street

LUCY	LOOMIS	DAVEY	SIRE	HORSE
SALLY	VARGAS	EDNA	ZEZE	MANGO
GERALDO	BUICK	FREE SPACE	TREES	MEME
MARIN	PAULINA	MUSIC	BENNY	LUPE
BOBO	MINERVA	ROSA	GRANDMOTHER	BIKE

House on Mango Street

DARIUS	RAFAELA	PUERTO	NENNY	MAGDALENA
GIL	NACHO	ELENITA	CATHY	EARL
HEELS	CADILLAC	FREE SPACE	RACHEL	MAMACITA
ALICIA	KEELER	ESPERANZA	MONKEY	MEXICAN
CANTEEN	LOIS	CORDERO	SISTERS	BIKE

House on Mango Street

BUICK	MONKEY	DAVEY	LUPE	GIL
BOBO	NACHO	GRANDMOTHER	RACHEL	ALICIA
ESPERANZA	CORDERO	FREE SPACE	TREES	PUERTO
EDNA	BIKE	EARL	CANTEEN	SIRE
BENNY	BABY	MANGO	PAULINA	ROSA

House on Mango Street

HORSE	RUTHIE	CADILLAC	NENNY	HEELS
MINERVA	LUCY	MAMACITA	SALLY	CATHY
KEELER	ZEZE	FREE SPACE	SISTERS	MEXICAN
LOOMIS	RAFAELA	DARIUS	MARIN	LOIS
MUSIC	MAGDALENA	GERALDO	MEME	ROSA

House on Mango Street

MINERVA	MEXICAN	RACHEL	CORDERO	MONKEY
GIL	RAFAELA	LUCY	ELENITA	NENNY
LUPE	HEELS	FREE SPACE	ESPERANZA	NACHO
ZEZE	ROSA	ALICIA	MEME	PAULINA
EDNA	LOOMIS	MUSIC	CADILLAC	CATHY

House on Mango Street

KEELER	SALLY	DARIUS	SISTERS	MAGDALENA
MAMACITA	SIRE	HORSE	BUICK	GRANDMOTHER
GERALDO	MANGO	FREE SPACE	PUERTO	EARL
LOIS	BENNY	DAVEY	VARGAS	BIKE
TREES	BABY	RUTHIE	MARIN	CATHY

House on Mango Street

KEELER	EDNA	MAMACITA	GRANDMOTHER	MAGDALENA
MANGO	BENNY	BOBO	SALLY	MONKEY
EARL	SIRE	FREE SPACE	HORSE	NACHO
ELENITA	MINERVA	TREES	ZEZE	GIL
LOOMIS	CATHY	BUICK	PAULINA	CADILLAC

House on Mango Street

BIKE	MEXICAN	ESPERANZA	VARGAS	PUERTO
DAVEY	HEELS	NENNY	CANTEEN	ALICIA
LUPE	RUTHIE	FREE SPACE	CORDERO	LUCY
BABY	MUSIC	MEME	GERALDO	ROSA
DARIUS	RAFAELA	LOIS	MARIN	CADILLAC

House on Mango Street

PUERTO	NENNY	CATHY	LUCY	PAULINA
ELENITA	EARL	CORDERO	DAVEY	MONKEY
CANTEEN	MEME	FREE SPACE	LOIS	GIL
MEXICAN	ZEZE	CADILLAC	HEELS	DARIUS
ESPERANZA	SALLY	NACHO	LUPE	MARIN

House on Mango Street

MAGDALENA	MINERVA	MAMACITA	SISTERS	HORSE
BABY	LOOMIS	RAFAELA	RUTHIE	GRANDMOTHER
GERALDO	ALICIA	FREE SPACE	MANGO	EDNA
BUICK	KEELER	VARGAS	ROSA	MUSIC
TREES	BENNY	RACHEL	SIRE	MARIN

House on Mango Street

EDNA	LUPE	RUTHIE	ESPERANZA	NACHO
MARIN	PAULINA	SALLY	BENNY	ROSA
CORDERO	MUSIC	FREE SPACE	GIL	CADILLAC
LOOMIS	MINERVA	MAMACITA	MEME	DAVEY
TREES	ZEZE	KEELER	RAFAELA	DARIUS

House on Mango Street

ELENITA	LOIS	VARGAS	GERALDO	MANGO
CATHY	LUCY	BOBO	MAGDALENA	GRANDMOTHER
BABY	BIKE	FREE SPACE	BUICK	PUERTO
EARL	MONKEY	CANTEEN	NENNY	MEXICAN
HEELS	ALICIA	HORSE	SISTERS	DARIUS

House on Mango Street

LOIS	PAULINA	EARL	LOOMIS	DAVEY
RUTHIE	MAMACITA	NENNY	BIKE	CANTEEN
BUICK	GRANDMOTHER	FREE SPACE	PUERTO	CATHY
BOBO	MAGDALENA	SIRE	DARIUS	MONKEY
MINERVA	SALLY	ZEZE	RACHEL	ELENITA

House on Mango Street

HORSE	NACHO	MEXICAN	CADILLAC	GERALDO
KEELER	GIL	ESPERANZA	SISTERS	ALICIA
MUSIC	BABY	FREE SPACE	TREES	HEELS
RAFAELA	CORDERO	ROSA	LUPE	LUCY
VARGAS	MEME	EDNA	BENNY	ELENITA

House on Mango Street

ZEZE	VARGAS	MANGO	NACHO	ROSA
KEELER	CATHY	GERALDO	ESPERANZA	LOIS
SISTERS	MEXICAN	FREE SPACE	BENNY	BOBO
MEME	RACHEL	BABY	SALLY	PAULINA
LUCY	MONKEY	ALICIA	MARIN	DAVEY

House on Mango Street

RAFAELA	MINERVA	RUTHIE	MAGDALENA	LUPE
GRANDMOTHER	HEELS	EDNA	BIKE	MUSIC
CORDERO	BUICK	FREE SPACE	CANTEEN	NENNY
LOOMIS	MAMACITA	SIRE	HORSE	CADILLAC
GIL	TREES	DARIUS	ELENITA	DAVEY

House on Mango Street

LUCY	GERALDO	CORDERO	LOIS	MARIN
CATHY	BIKE	LUPE	HORSE	MAGDALENA
KEELER	NACHO	FREE SPACE	CADILLAC	MONKEY
MEXICAN	ZEZE	ALICIA	NENNY	LOOMIS
BENNY	PAULINA	MINERVA	GIL	MUSIC

House on Mango Street

SIRE	PUERTO	BABY	CANTEEN	TREES
GRANDMOTHER	BUICK	RUTHIE	DAVEY	EARL
RACHEL	MANGO	FREE SPACE	DARIUS	RAFAELA
EDNA	ELENITA	VARGAS	MEME	SALLY
ROSA	BOBO	SISTERS	ESPERANZA	MUSIC

House on Mango Street

MEXICAN	BABY	BOBO	SALLY	LOOMIS
KEELER	MAGDALENA	DAVEY	SIRE	ESPERANZA
ELENITA	HORSE	FREE SPACE	VARGAS	HEELS
ZEZE	DARIUS	BIKE	SISTERS	BUICK
EDNA	GIL	MEME	CATHY	MINERVA

House on Mango Street

LUPE	ALICIA	PAULINA	CANTEEN	NENNY
MONKEY	LUCY	RACHEL	ROSA	RAFAELA
MANGO	GERALDO	FREE SPACE	GRANDMOTHER	TREES
PUERTO	LOIS	CADILLAC	EARL	RUTHIE
CORDERO	MUSIC	NACHO	MAMACITA	MINERVA

House on Mango Street

NENNY	SIRE	MANGO	MAGDALENA	SISTERS
VARGAS	CORDERO	MEXICAN	MEME	MAMACITA
ESPERANZA	BOBO	FREE SPACE	TREES	BABY
HEELS	LOIS	MONKEY	MINERVA	EARL
PUERTO	DAVEY	BUICK	KEELER	ELENITA

House on Mango Street

LUPE	BENNY	PAULINA	ALICIA	SALLY
LUCY	HORSE	ROSA	CATHY	RACHEL
LOOMIS	MARIN	FREE SPACE	CANTEEN	RUTHIE
EDNA	RAFAELA	CADILLAC	DARIUS	GERALDO
BIKE	NACHO	ZEZE	GRANDMOTHER	ELENITA

House on Mango Street

DAVEY	TREES	SALLY	MINERVA	SIRE
LOOMIS	RACHEL	MAGDALENA	GERALDO	MEME
MUSIC	RUTHIE	FREE SPACE	CANTEEN	BUICK
CORDERO	RAFAELA	ELENITA	KEELER	MAMACITA
GRANDMOTHER	NACHO	ALICIA	ZEZE	LOIS

House on Mango Street

SISTERS	BOBO	MANGO	DARIUS	BABY
PUERTO	MEXICAN	LUCY	GIL	VARGAS
EARL	BENNY	FREE SPACE	ESPERANZA	HEELS
MONKEY	BIKE	CADILLAC	NENNY	MARIN
EDNA	PAULINA	ROSA	HORSE	LOIS

House on Mango Street

CATHY	CADILLAC	GERALDO	LOIS	TREES
MONKEY	ESPERANZA	MEXICAN	RACHEL	SISTERS
MINERVA	MARIN	FREE SPACE	MEME	ALICIA
EDNA	RAFAELA	BENNY	CANTEEN	MAGDALENA
GRANDMOTHER	DARIUS	RUTHIE	BUICK	MANGO

House on Mango Street

LOOMIS	SIRE	NENNY	NACHO	MAMACITA
ZEZE	HEELS	DAVEY	PUERTO	GIL
BOBO	BABY	FREE SPACE	VARGAS	HORSE
BIKE	LUPE	LUCY	ROSA	MUSIC
SALLY	PAULINA	CORDERO	KEELER	MANGO

House on Mango Street

NENNY	DARIUS	NACHO	CANTEEN	MEXICAN
MARIN	SISTERS	BOBO	MAGDALENA	GERALDO
CADILLAC	MEME	FREE SPACE	HORSE	VARGAS
LOIS	SIRE	EDNA	BIKE	DAVEY
GRANDMOTHER	KEELER	MINERVA	MANGO	EARL

House on Mango Street

HEELS	CORDERO	CATHY	MONKEY	PAULINA
LOOMIS	ELENITA	ZEZE	RUTHIE	BUICK
ROSA	LUCY	FREE SPACE	GIL	SALLY
TREES	BENNY	PUERTO	ESPERANZA	LUPE
MAMACITA	BABY	ALICIA	MUSIC	EARL

House on Mango Street

MUSIC	LOIS	PUERTO	MARIN	BOBO
SISTERS	MAGDALENA	GERALDO	MEME	ELENITA
MINERVA	SIRE	FREE SPACE	PAULINA	DAVEY
SALLY	CANTEEN	BABY	ESPERANZA	TREES
NACHO	RAFAELA	MAMACITA	KEELER	MEXICAN

House on Mango Street

BENNY	EARL	BIKE	RACHEL	DARIUS
MANGO	GRANDMOTHER	NENNY	LUPE	HEELS
VARGAS	CORDERO	FREE SPACE	CADILLAC	MONKEY
ZEZE	LOOMIS	CATHY	ROSA	RUTHIE
EDNA	BUICK	GIL	HORSE	MEXICAN

House on Mango Street Vocabulary Word List

No.	Word	Clue/Definition
1.	AISLES	Passageways in a store or theater
2.	ANCHOR	Heavy object used to keep a boat in place
3.	ANEMIC	Weak; without much energy
4.	ANNUAL	Done every year
5.	ATTIC	A room directly below the roof
6.	AUTOMATICALLY	Done by machine
7.	BAPTIZE	To give a first or Christian name to
8.	BAZAAR	A fair or sale
9.	CANTEEN	A small cafeteria or snack bar
10.	CAPSULES	Small, oval shaped, jelly-like container
11.	CHANDELIER	A light fixture that hangs from a ceiling
12.	COMPLICATED	Not easy to understand
13.	CONTENT	Satisfied
14.	CUMULUS	White, fluffy clouds with a flat base
15.	CURRENCY	Money
16.	DESCENDED	Went down
17.	DISTANT	Far apart in relationship
18.	FEROCIOUS	Savage, fierce
19.	FLATS	Apartments all on one floor
20.	FLECKS	Tiny spots
21.	GOBLETS	Glasses with stems and bases
22.	HYDRANT	An upright cylinder for holding water
23.	HYSTERICAL	Uncontrolled laughing or crying
24.	IGNITION	The switch that turns on a car
25.	INHERIT	To receive from one who has gone before
26.	INTERN	An advanced student
27.	LINOLEUM	A washable floor covering
28.	LUXURY	Comfort and pleasure
29.	MARIMBAS	Wooden, xylophone-like instruments
30.	NAPHTHA	A kind of soap
31.	NIMBUS	A low, dark rain cloud
32.	PILLAR	A column or vertical support
33.	PLUCKED	Removed with the fingers
34.	PLUNGERS	Rubber suction cups on sticks
35.	RAVEN	A large bird with black feathers
36.	RESPONSIBILITY	Duty
37.	SLANT	Slope; go in a diagonal direction
38.	SLATS	Narrow strips of wood or metal
39.	STRUTTED	Walked in a pompous way; swaggered
40.	SURGEON	A doctor who operates on patients
41.	TEMPORARY	For a limited time
42.	THRESHOLD	An entrance or doorway
43.	TRUDGED	Walked in a heavy-footed way; plodded
44.	TWANGY	A sharp, vibrating sound

House on Mango Street Vocabulary Fill In The Blank 1

_____ 1. Comfort and pleasure

_____ 2. Glasses with stems and bases

_____ 3. A light fixture that hangs from a ceiling

_____ 4. Wooden, xylophone-like instruments

_____ 5. For a limited time

_____ 6. Satisfied

_____ 7. Removed with the fingers

_____ 8. An upright cylinder for holding water

_____ 9. Uncontrolled laughing or crying

_____ 10. Money

_____ 11. A fair or sale

_____ 12. Narrow strips of wood or metal

_____ 13. A column or vertical support

_____ 14. Done every year

_____ 15. Small, oval shaped, jelly-like container

_____ 16. Savage, fierce

_____ 17. A kind of soap

_____ 18. Done by machine

_____ 19. A small cafeteria or snack bar

_____ 20. A large bird with black feathers

House on Mango Street Vocabulary Fil In The Blank 1 Answer Key

LUXURY	1. Comfort and pleasure
GOBLETS	2. Glasses with stems and bases
CHANDELIER	3. A light fixture that hangs from a ceiling
MARIMBAS	4. Wooden, xylophone-like instruments
TEMPORARY	5. For a limited time
CONTENT	6. Satisfied
PLUCKED	7. Removed with the fingers
HYDRANT	8. An upright cylinder for holding water
HYSTERICAL	9. Uncontrolled laughing or crying
CURRENCY	10. Money
BAZAAR	11. A fair or sale
SLATS	12. Narrow strips of wood or metal
PILLAR	13. A column or vertical support
ANNUAL	14. Done every year
CAPSULES	15. Small, oval shaped, jelly-like container
FEROCIOUS	16. Savage, fierce
NAPHTHA	17. A kind of soap
AUTOMATICALLY	18. Done by machine
CANTEEN	19. A small cafeteria or snack bar
RAVEN	20. A large bird with black feathers

House on Mango Street Vocabulary Fill In The Blank 2

_____ 1. Uncontrolled laughing or crying

_____ 2. Removed with the fingers

_____ 3. Done by machine

_____ 4. Savage, fierce

_____ 5. Far apart in relationship

_____ 6. A column or vertical support

_____ 7. Rubber suction cups on sticks

_____ 8. Glasses with stems and bases

_____ 9. Satisfied

_____ 10. Not easy to understand

_____ 11. A small cafeteria or snack bar

_____ 12. Slope; go in a diagonal direction

_____ 13. A room directly below the roof

_____ 14. An entrance or doorway

_____ 15. To receive from one who has gone before

_____ 16. A light fixture that hangs from a ceiling

_____ 17. A kind of soap

_____ 18. A washable floor covering

_____ 19. Walked in a heavy-footed way; plodded

_____ 20. Done every year

House on Mango Street Vocabulary Fill In The Blank 2 Answer Key

HYSTERICAL	1.	Uncontrolled laughing or crying
PLUCKED	2.	Removed with the fingers
AUTOMATICALLY	3.	Done by machine
FEROCIOUS	4.	Savage, fierce
DISTANT	5.	Far apart in relationship
PILLAR	6.	A column or vertical support
PLUNGERS	7.	Rubber suction cups on sticks
GOBLETS	8.	Glasses with stems and bases
CONTENT	9.	Satisfied
COMPLICATED	10.	Not easy to understand
CANTEEN	11.	A small cafeteria or snack bar
SLANT	12.	Slope; go in a diagonal direction
ATTIC	13.	A room directly below the roof
THRESHOLD	14.	An entrance or doorway
INHERIT	15.	To receive from one who has gone before
CHANDELIER	16.	A light fixture that hangs from a ceiling
NAPHTHA	17.	A kind of soap
LINOLEUM	18.	A washable floor covering
TRUDGED	19.	Walked in a heavy-footed way; plodded
ANNUAL	20.	Done every year

House on Mango Street Vocabulary Fill In The Blank 3

_____ 1. A low, dark rain cloud

_____ 2. Done by machine

_____ 3. Apartments all on one floor

_____ 4. A doctor who operates on patients

_____ 5. Done every year

_____ 6. A large bird with black feathers

_____ 7. A fair or sale

_____ 8. The switch that turns on a car

_____ 9. Comfort and pleasure

_____ 10. Walked in a pompous way; swaggered

_____ 11. Removed with the fingers

_____ 12. Walked in a heavy-footed way; plodded

_____ 13. A kind of soap

_____ 14. Narrow strips of wood or metal

_____ 15. A washable floor covering

_____ 16. Went down

_____ 17. To give a first or Christian name to

_____ 18. A light fixture that hangs from a ceiling

_____ 19. Wooden, xylophone-like instruments

_____ 20. Uncontrolled laughing or crying

House on Mango Street Vocabulary Fill In The Blank 3 Answer Key

NIMBUS	1. A low, dark rain cloud
AUTOMATICALLY	2. Done by machine
FLATS	3. Apartments all on one floor
SURGEON	4. A doctor who operates on patients
ANNUAL	5. Done every year
RAVEN	6. A large bird with black feathers
BAZAAR	7. A fair or sale
IGNITION	8. The switch that turns on a car
LUXURY	9. Comfort and pleasure
STRUTTED	10. Walked in a pompous way; swaggered
PLUCKED	11. Removed with the fingers
TRUDGED	12. Walked in a heavy-footed way; plodded
NAPHTHA	13. A kind of soap
SLATS	14. Narrow strips of wood or metal
LINOLEUM	15. A washable floor covering
DESCENDED	16. Went down
BAPTIZE	17. To give a first or Christian name to
CHANDELIER	18. A light fixture that hangs from a ceiling
MARIMBAS	19. Wooden, xylophone-like instruments
HYSTERICAL	20. Uncontrolled laughing or crying

House on Mango Street Vocabulary Fill In The Blank 4

1. A doctor who operates on patients
2. Satisfied
3. A low, dark rain cloud
4. Removed with the fingers
5. Done every year
6. Tiny spots
7. Heavy object used to keep a boat in place
8. An advanced student
9. To give a first or Christian name to
10. Done by machine
11. White, fluffy clouds with a flat base
12. Went down
13. Passageways in a store or theater
14. Money
15. Not easy to understand
16. A kind of soap
17. A fair or sale
18. A light fixture that hangs from a ceiling
19. Rubber suction cups on sticks
20. Savage, fierce

House on Mango Street Vocabulary Fill In The Blank 4 Answer Key

SURGEON	1. A doctor who operates on patients
CONTENT	2. Satisfied
NIMBUS	3. A low, dark rain cloud
PLUCKED	4. Removed with the fingers
ANNUAL	5. Done every year
FLECKS	6. Tiny spots
ANCHOR	7. Heavy object used to keep a boat in place
INTERN	8. An advanced student
BAPTIZE	9. To give a first or Christian name to
AUTOMATICALLY	10. Done by machine
CUMULUS	11. White, fluffy clouds with a flat base
DESCENDED	12. Went down
AISLES	13. Passageways in a store or theater
CURRENCY	14. Money
COMPLICATED	15. Not easy to understand
NAPHTHA	16. A kind of soap
BAZAAR	17. A fair or sale
CHANDELIER	18. A light fixture that hangs from a ceiling
PLUNGERS	19. Rubber suction cups on sticks
FEROCIOUS	20. Savage, fierce

House on Mango Street Vocabulary Matching 1

___ 1. PLUCKED   A. Wooden, xylophone-like instruments
___ 2. NAPHTHA   B. Rubber suction cups on sticks
___ 3. ANCHOR   C. White, fluffy clouds with a flat base
___ 4. AISLES   D. A washable floor covering
___ 5. CAPSULES   E. Small, oval shaped, jelly-like container
___ 6. RESPONSIBILITY   F. Walked in a heavy-footed way; plodded
___ 7. AUTOMATICALLY   G. To receive from one who has gone before
___ 8. GOBLETS   H. Done by machine
___ 9. FEROCIOUS   I. An upright cylinder for holding water
___10. FLECKS   J. Went down
___11. TRUDGED   K. Passageways in a store or theater
___12. PLUNGERS   L. Heavy object used to keep a boat in place
___13. CURRENCY   M. Slope; go in a diagonal direction
___14. SLANT   N. A kind of soap
___15. INHERIT   O. Money
___16. FLATS   P. Savage, fierce
___17. DISTANT   Q. Walked in a pompous way; swaggered
___18. CUMULUS   R. Glasses with stems and bases
___19. HYDRANT   S. Duty
___20. LUXURY   T. Apartments all on one floor
___21. MARIMBAS   U. Removed with the fingers
___22. BAPTIZE   V. To give a first or Christian name to
___23. DESCENDED   W. Comfort and pleasure
___24. LINOLEUM   X. Tiny spots
___25. STRUTTED   Y. Far apart in relationship

House on Mango Street Vocabulary Matching 1 Answer Key

U - 1. PLUCKED	A.	Wooden, xylophone-like instruments
N - 2. NAPHTHA	B.	Rubber suction cups on sticks
L - 3. ANCHOR	C.	White, fluffy clouds with a flat base
K - 4. AISLES	D.	A washable floor covering
E - 5. CAPSULES	E.	Small, oval shaped, jelly-like container
S - 6. RESPONSIBILITY	F.	Walked in a heavy-footed way; plodded
H - 7. AUTOMATICALLY	G.	To receive from one who has gone before
R - 8. GOBLETS	H.	Done by machine
P - 9. FEROCIOUS	I.	An upright cylinder for holding water
X -10. FLECKS	J.	Went down
F -11. TRUDGED	K.	Passageways in a store or theater
B -12. PLUNGERS	L.	Heavy object used to keep a boat in place
O -13. CURRENCY	M.	Slope; go in a diagonal direction
M -14. SLANT	N.	A kind of soap
G -15. INHERIT	O.	Money
T -16. FLATS	P.	Savage, fierce
Y -17. DISTANT	Q.	Walked in a pompous way; swaggered
C -18. CUMULUS	R.	Glasses with stems and bases
I - 19. HYDRANT	S.	Duty
W -20. LUXURY	T.	Apartments all on one floor
A -21. MARIMBAS	U.	Removed with the fingers
V -22. BAPTIZE	V.	To give a first or Christian name to
J - 23. DESCENDED	W.	Comfort and pleasure
D -24. LINOLEUM	X.	Tiny spots
Q -25. STRUTTED	Y.	Far apart in relationship

Copyrighted

House on Mango Street Vocabulary Matching 2

___ 1. LINOLEUM   A. Wooden, xylophone-like instruments
___ 2. FEROCIOUS   B. Slope; go in a diagonal direction
___ 3. TEMPORARY   C. The switch that turns on a car
___ 4. NIMBUS   D. Small, oval shaped, jelly-like container
___ 5. RESPONSIBILITY   E. Not easy to understand
___ 6. STRUTTED   F. A low, dark rain cloud
___ 7. DISTANT   G. A column or vertical support
___ 8. ANCHOR   H. Glasses with stems and bases
___ 9. LUXURY   I. White, fluffy clouds with a flat base
___10. SLANT   J. Walked in a heavy-footed way; plodded
___11. CAPSULES   K. Apartments all on one floor
___12. INTERN   L. Comfort and pleasure
___13. COMPLICATED   M. An upright cylinder for holding water
___14. CHANDELIER   N. A light fixture that hangs from a ceiling
___15. SLATS   O. Walked in a pompous way; swaggered
___16. FLATS   P. Heavy object used to keep a boat in place
___17. TWANGY   Q. An advanced student
___18. DESCENDED   R. Far apart in relationship
___19. HYDRANT   S. Narrow strips of wood or metal
___20. GOBLETS   T. Duty
___21. PILLAR   U. A washable floor covering
___22. TRUDGED   V. A sharp, vibrating sound
___23. CUMULUS   W. Went down
___24. IGNITION   X. Savage, fierce
___25. MARIMBAS   Y. For a limited time

House on Mango Street Vocabulary Matching 2 Answer Key

U - 1. LINOLEUM	A.	Wooden, xylophone-like instruments
X - 2. FEROCIOUS	B.	Slope; go in a diagonal direction
Y - 3. TEMPORARY	C.	The switch that turns on a car
F - 4. NIMBUS	D.	Small, oval shaped, jelly-like container
T - 5. RESPONSIBILITY	E.	Not easy to understand
O - 6. STRUTTED	F.	A low, dark rain cloud
R - 7. DISTANT	G.	A column or vertical support
P - 8. ANCHOR	H.	Glasses with stems and bases
L - 9. LUXURY	I.	White, fluffy clouds with a flat base
B - 10. SLANT	J.	Walked in a heavy-footed way; plodded
D - 11. CAPSULES	K.	Apartments all on one floor
Q - 12. INTERN	L.	Comfort and pleasure
E - 13. COMPLICATED	M.	An upright cylinder for holding water
N - 14. CHANDELIER	N.	A light fixture that hangs from a ceiling
S - 15. SLATS	O.	Walked in a pompous way; swaggered
K - 16. FLATS	P.	Heavy object used to keep a boat in place
V - 17. TWANGY	Q.	An advanced student
W - 18. DESCENDED	R.	Far apart in relationship
M - 19. HYDRANT	S.	Narrow strips of wood or metal
H - 20. GOBLETS	T.	Duty
G - 21. PILLAR	U.	A washable floor covering
J - 22. TRUDGED	V.	A sharp, vibrating sound
I - 23. CUMULUS	W.	Went down
C - 24. IGNITION	X.	Savage, fierce
A - 25. MARIMBAS	Y.	For a limited time

House on Mango Street Vocabulary Matching 3

___ 1. PLUNGERS   A. Rubber suction cups on sticks
___ 2. FLECKS   B. Uncontrolled laughing or crying
___ 3. NIMBUS   C. Removed with the fingers
___ 4. PILLAR   D. White, fluffy clouds with a flat base
___ 5. STRUTTED   E. Walked in a pompous way; swaggered
___ 6. THRESHOLD   F. Glasses with stems and bases
___ 7. CUMULUS   G. For a limited time
___ 8. IGNITION   H. Satisfied
___ 9. LUXURY   I. Savage, fierce
___10. FLATS   J. Passageways in a store or theater
___11. TEMPORARY   K. The switch that turns on a car
___12. GOBLETS   L. A kind of soap
___13. PLUCKED   M. An entrance or doorway
___14. ANNUAL   N. Comfort and pleasure
___15. NAPHTHA   O. Done every year
___16. RESPONSIBILITY   P. A low, dark rain cloud
___17. ATTIC   Q. To give a first or Christian name to
___18. CONTENT   R. A sharp, vibrating sound
___19. FEROCIOUS   S. Tiny spots
___20. AUTOMATICALLY   T. A room directly below the roof
___21. HYSTERICAL   U. Done by machine
___22. TWANGY   V. Duty
___23. AISLES   W. A column or vertical support
___24. BAPTIZE   X. A washable floor covering
___25. LINOLEUM   Y. Apartments all on one floor

House on Mango Street Vocabulary Matching 3 Answer Key

A - 1. PLUNGERS	A.	Rubber suction cups on sticks
S - 2. FLECKS	B.	Uncontrolled laughing or crying
P - 3. NIMBUS	C.	Removed with the fingers
W - 4. PILLAR	D.	White, fluffy clouds with a flat base
E - 5. STRUTTED	E.	Walked in a pompous way; swaggered
M - 6. THRESHOLD	F.	Glasses with stems and bases
D - 7. CUMULUS	G.	For a limited time
K - 8. IGNITION	H.	Satisfied
N - 9. LUXURY	I.	Savage, fierce
Y -10. FLATS	J.	Passageways in a store or theater
G -11. TEMPORARY	K.	The switch that turns on a car
F -12. GOBLETS	L.	A kind of soap
C -13. PLUCKED	M.	An entrance or doorway
O -14. ANNUAL	N.	Comfort and pleasure
L -15. NAPHTHA	O.	Done every year
V -16. RESPONSIBILITY	P.	A low, dark rain cloud
T -17. ATTIC	Q.	To give a first or Christian name to
H -18. CONTENT	R.	A sharp, vibrating sound
I -19. FEROCIOUS	S.	Tiny spots
U -20. AUTOMATICALLY	T.	A room directly below the roof
B -21. HYSTERICAL	U.	Done by machine
R -22. TWANGY	V.	Duty
J -23. AISLES	W.	A column or vertical support
Q -24. BAPTIZE	X.	A washable floor covering
X -25. LINOLEUM	Y.	Apartments all on one floor

House on Mango Street Vocabulary Matching 4

___ 1. BAPTIZE   A. A fair or sale
___ 2. GOBLETS   B. Not easy to understand
___ 3. HYSTERICAL   C. Removed with the fingers
___ 4. BAZAAR   D. Apartments all on one floor
___ 5. PLUNGERS   E. Far apart in relationship
___ 6. FEROCIOUS   F. The switch that turns on a car
___ 7. LUXURY   G. Duty
___ 8. RESPONSIBILITY   H. Small, oval shaped, jelly-like container
___ 9. THRESHOLD   I. A light fixture that hangs from a ceiling
___10. FLATS   J. Walked in a pompous way; swaggered
___11. CHANDELIER   K. Tiny spots
___12. DISTANT   L. To give a first or Christian name to
___13. ANNUAL   M. Rubber suction cups on sticks
___14. FLECKS   N. A doctor who operates on patients
___15. NAPHTHA   O. Heavy object used to keep a boat in place
___16. INHERIT   P. A kind of soap
___17. CAPSULES   Q. To receive from one who has gone before
___18. SURGEON   R. Narrow strips of wood or metal
___19. CUMULUS   S. An entrance or doorway
___20. PLUCKED   T. White, fluffy clouds with a flat base
___21. STRUTTED   U. Glasses with stems and bases
___22. IGNITION   V. Uncontrolled laughing or crying
___23. ANCHOR   W. Savage, fierce
___24. SLATS   X. Done every year
___25. COMPLICATED   Y. Comfort and pleasure

House on Mango Street Vocabulary Matching 4 Answer Key

L - 1. BAPTIZE
U - 2. GOBLETS
V - 3. HYSTERICAL
A - 4. BAZAAR
M - 5. PLUNGERS
W - 6. FEROCIOUS
Y - 7. LUXURY
G - 8. RESPONSIBILITY
S - 9. THRESHOLD
D - 10. FLATS
I - 11. CHANDELIER
E - 12. DISTANT
X - 13. ANNUAL
K - 14. FLECKS
P - 15. NAPHTHA
Q - 16. INHERIT
H - 17. CAPSULES
N - 18. SURGEON
T - 19. CUMULUS
C - 20. PLUCKED
J - 21. STRUTTED
F - 22. IGNITION
O - 23. ANCHOR
R - 24. SLATS
B - 25. COMPLICATED

A. A fair or sale
B. Not easy to understand
C. Removed with the fingers
D. Apartments all on one floor
E. Far apart in relationship
F. The switch that turns on a car
G. Duty
H. Small, oval shaped, jelly-like container
I. A light fixture that hangs from a ceiling
J. Walked in a pompous way; swaggered
K. Tiny spots
L. To give a first or Christian name to
M. Rubber suction cups on sticks
N. A doctor who operates on patients
O. Heavy object used to keep a boat in place
P. A kind of soap
Q. To receive from one who has gone before
R. Narrow strips of wood or metal
S. An entrance or doorway
T. White, fluffy clouds with a flat base
U. Glasses with stems and bases
V. Uncontrolled laughing or crying
W. Savage, fierce
X. Done every year
Y. Comfort and pleasure

House on Mango Street Vocabulary Magic Squares 1

Match the definition with the vocabulary word. Put your answers in the magic squares below. When your answers are correct, all columns and rows will add to the same number.

A. PLUNGERS
B. DISTANT
C. NIMBUS
D. CAPSULES
E. LINOLEUM
F. ATTIC
G. STRUTTED
H. CANTEEN
I. NAPHTHA
J. BAZAAR
K. ANNUAL
L. CHANDELIER
M. AISLES
N. PILLAR
O. SLANT
P. BAPTIZE

1. Slope; go in a diagonal direction
2. Small, oval shaped, jelly-like container
3. A fair or sale
4. A washable floor covering
5. A kind of soap
6. A room directly below the roof
7. To give a first or Christian name to
8. A low, dark rain cloud
9. A small cafeteria or snack bar
10. Done every year
11. Rubber suction cups on sticks
12. A column or vertical support
13. Far apart in relationship
14. Passageways in a store or theater
15. Walked in a pompous way; swaggered
16. A light fixture that hangs from a ceiling

A=	B=	C=	D=
E=	F=	G=	H=
I=	J=	K=	L=
M=	N=	O=	P=

House on Mango Street Vocabulary Magic Squares 1 Answer Key

Match the definition with the vocabulary word. Put your answers in the magic squares below. When your answers are correct, all columns and rows will add to the same number.

A. PLUNGERS
B. DISTANT
C. NIMBUS
D. CAPSULES
E. LINOLEUM
F. ATTIC
G. STRUTTED
H. CANTEEN
I. NAPHTHA
J. BAZAAR
K. ANNUAL
L. CHANDELIER
M. AISLES
N. PILLAR
O. SLANT
P. BAPTIZE

1. Slope; go in a diagonal direction
2. Small, oval shaped, jelly-like container
3. A fair or sale
4. A washable floor covering
5. A kind of soap
6. A room directly below the roof
7. To give a first or Christian name to
8. A low, dark rain cloud
9. A small cafeteria or snack bar
10. Done every year
11. Rubber suction cups on sticks
12. A column or vertical support
13. Far apart in relationship
14. Passageways in a store or theater
15. Walked in a pompous way; swaggered
16. A light fixture that hangs from a ceiling

A=11	B=13	C=8	D=2
E=4	F=6	G=15	H=9
I=5	J=3	K=10	L=16
M=14	N=12	O=1	P=7

House on Mango Street Vocabulary Magic Squares 2

Match the definition with the vocabulary word. Put your answers in the magic squares below. When your answers are correct, all columns and rows will add to the same number.

A. DISTANT
B. AISLES
C. SLATS
D. TRUDGED
E. FEROCIOUS
F. BAPTIZE
G. HYSTERICAL
H. AUTOMATICALLY
I. HYDRANT
J. THRESHOLD
K. GOBLETS
L. CUMULUS
M. MARIMBAS
N. SURGEON
O. STRUTTED
P. PLUNGERS

1. Narrow strips of wood or metal
2. An entrance or doorway
3. To give a first or Christian name to
4. Walked in a pompous way; swaggered
5. Rubber suction cups on sticks
6. Savage, fierce
7. An upright cylinder for holding water
8. Walked in a heavy-footed way; plodded
9. Wooden, xylophone-like instruments
10. Done by machine
11. White, fluffy clouds with a flat base
12. Far apart in relationship
13. Passageways in a store or theater
14. Glasses with stems and bases
15. Uncontrolled laughing or crying
16. A doctor who operates on patients

A=	B=	C=	D=
E=	F=	G=	H=
I=	J=	K=	L=
M=	N=	O=	P=

House on Mango Street Vocabulary Magic Squares 2 Answer Key

Match the definition with the vocabulary word. Put your answers in the magic squares below. When your answers are correct, all columns and rows will add to the same number.

A. DISTANT
B. AISLES
C. SLATS
D. TRUDGED
E. FEROCIOUS
F. BAPTIZE
G. HYSTERICAL
H. AUTOMATICALLY
I. HYDRANT
J. THRESHOLD
K. GOBLETS
L. CUMULUS
M. MARIMBAS
N. SURGEON
O. STRUTTED
P. PLUNGERS

1. Narrow strips of wood or metal
2. An entrance or doorway
3. To give a first or Christian name to
4. Walked in a pompous way; swaggered
5. Rubber suction cups on sticks
6. Savage, fierce
7. An upright cylinder for holding water
8. Walked in a heavy-footed way; plodded
9. Wooden, xylophone-like instruments
10. Done by machine
11. White, fluffy clouds with a flat base
12. Far apart in relationship
13. Passageways in a store or theater
14. Glasses with stems and bases
15. Uncontrolled laughing or crying
16. A doctor who operates on patients

A=12	B=13	C=1	D=8
E=6	F=3	G=15	H=10
I=7	J=2	K=14	L=11
M=9	N=16	O=4	P=5

House on Mango Street Vocabulary Magic Squares 3

Match the definition with the vocabulary word. Put your answers in the magic squares below. When your answers are correct, all columns and rows will add to the same number.

A. CUMULUS
B. PLUNGERS
C. LINOLEUM
D. IGNITION
E. SURGEON
F. INHERIT
G. CURRENCY
H. SLANT
I. FEROCIOUS
J. ATTIC
K. FLECKS
L. RAVEN
M. MARIMBAS
N. BAPTIZE
O. AISLES
P. CANTEEN

1. White, fluffy clouds with a flat base
2. To give a first or Christian name to
3. A room directly below the roof
4. A doctor who operates on patients
5. Money
6. A large bird with black feathers
7. A small cafeteria or snack bar
8. A washable floor covering
9. Passageways in a store or theater
10. The switch that turns on a car
11. Slope; go in a diagonal direction
12. Tiny spots
13. Savage, fierce
14. To receive from one who has gone before
15. Rubber suction cups on sticks
16. Wooden, xylophone-like instruments

A=	B=	C=	D=
E=	F=	G=	H=
I=	J=	K=	L=
M=	N=	O=	P=

House on Mango Street Vocabulary Magic Squares 3 Answer Key

Match the definition with the vocabulary word. Put your answers in the magic squares below. When your answers are correct, all columns and rows will add to the same number.

A. CUMULUS
B. PLUNGERS
C. LINOLEUM
D. IGNITION
E. SURGEON
F. INHERIT
G. CURRENCY
H. SLANT
I. FEROCIOUS
J. ATTIC
K. FLECKS
L. RAVEN
M. MARIMBAS
N. BAPTIZE
O. AISLES
P. CANTEEN

1. White, fluffy clouds with a flat base
2. To give a first or Christian name to
3. A room directly below the roof
4. A doctor who operates on patients
5. Money
6. A large bird with black feathers
7. A small cafeteria or snack bar
8. A washable floor covering
9. Passageways in a store or theater
10. The switch that turns on a car
11. Slope; go in a diagonal direction
12. Tiny spots
13. Savage, fierce
14. To receive from one who has gone before
15. Rubber suction cups on sticks
16. Wooden, xylophone-like instruments

A=1	B=15	C=8	D=10
E=4	F=14	G=5	H=11
I=13	J=3	K=12	L=6
M=16	N=2	O=9	P=7

House on Mango Street Vocabulary Magic Squares 4

Match the definition with the vocabulary word. Put your answers in the magic squares below. When your answers are correct, all columns and rows will add to the same number.

A. FEROCIOUS
B. TRUDGED
C. SURGEON
D. BAZAAR
E. CHANDELIER
F. PLUCKED
G. SLANT
H. BAPTIZE
I. NIMBUS
J. HYDRANT
K. AISLES
L. GOBLETS
M. PILLAR
N. FLECKS
O. CURRENCY
P. CUMULUS

1. Removed with the fingers
2. A low, dark rain cloud
3. Money
4. A fair or sale
5. A column or vertical support
6. Walked in a heavy-footed way; plodded
7. To give a first or Christian name to
8. Passageways in a store or theater
9. A doctor who operates on patients
10. White, fluffy clouds with a flat base
11. An upright cylinder for holding water
12. A light fixture that hangs from a ceiling
13. Glasses with stems and bases
14. Slope; go in a diagonal direction
15. Savage, fierce
16. Tiny spots

A=	B=	C=	D=
E=	F=	G=	H=
I=	J=	K=	L=
M=	N=	O=	P=

House on Mango Street Vocabulary Magic Squares 4 Answer Key

Match the definition with the vocabulary word. Put your answers in the magic squares below. When your answers are correct, all columns and rows will add to the same number.

A. FEROCIOUS
B. TRUDGED
C. SURGEON
D. BAZAAR
E. CHANDELIER
F. PLUCKED
G. SLANT
H. BAPTIZE
I. NIMBUS
J. HYDRANT
K. AISLES
L. GOBLETS
M. PILLAR
N. FLECKS
O. CURRENCY
P. CUMULUS

1. Removed with the fingers
2. A low, dark rain cloud
3. Money
4. A fair or sale
5. A column or vertical support
6. Walked in a heavy-footed way; plodded
7. To give a first or Christian name to
8. Passageways in a store or theater
9. A doctor who operates on patients
10. White, fluffy clouds with a flat base
11. An upright cylinder for holding water
12. A light fixture that hangs from a ceiling
13. Glasses with stems and bases
14. Slope; go in a diagonal direction
15. Savage, fierce
16. Tiny spots

A=15	B=6	C=9	D=4
E=12	F=1	G=14	H=7
I=2	J=11	K=8	L=13
M=5	N=16	O=3	P=10

House on Mango Street Vocabulary Word Search 1

```
C U M U L U S P Z Z X G G T M T N E T N O C
F L S M F F E R O C I O U S H W B N R S C V
H Y S T E R I C A L N B N J P A K E Z R V T
W R E S P O N S I B I L I T Y N Y V S E S C
Q S P D D E S C E N D E D C D G T A L G F C
T H R E S H O L D A T T I C H Y D R A N T C
N L Z G A P W E E L L S E G A R W N N U Q S
T X U R N L T D K I H D T M X N C G T L R K
Y M W X N T B I C G N E S S P H E S S P L G
C A P S U L E S U L W T V M O O Z M N D D K
N J F R A R N T L G A A E R A Z R O I E R R
E R T L L E Y A P L S C P R H R E A G C E B
R S P G E B Z N F N O I T I N G I D R I P Y
R B C T K C A T M L L H I R A U M L Y Z X
U N N N Z J K Z J L H P R U N R P E B S Q S
C A S L A T S S A K M M S H T H D H E A U S
C Y L V F Q K R W A F O L F Q N E L T B S S
P T Q D T X H L B K R C L G A L S R M H H S
B A P T I Z E Z C J B W B H L I R I I L A G
L I N O L E U M D K H J C J A L N D H T D B
```

A column or vertical support (6)
A doctor who operates on patients (7)
A fair or sale (6)
A kind of soap (7)
A large bird with black feathers (5)
A light fixture that hangs from a ceiling (10)
A low, dark rain cloud (6)
A room directly below the roof (5)
A sharp, vibrating sound (6)
A small cafeteria or snack bar (7)
A washable floor covering (8)
An advanced student (6)
An entrance or doorway (9)
An upright cylinder for holding water (7)
Apartments all on one floor (5)
Comfort and pleasure (6)
Done every year (6)
Duty (14)
Far apart in relationship (7)
For a limited time (9)
Glasses with stems and bases (7)
Heavy object used to keep a boat in place (6)
Money (8)

Narrow strips of wood or metal (5)
Not easy to understand (11)
Passageways in a store or theater (6)
Removed with the fingers (7)
Rubber suction cups on sticks (8)
Satisfied (7)
Savage, fierce (9)
Slope; go in a diagonal direction (5)
Small, oval shaped, jelly-like container (8)
The switch that turns on a car (8)
Tiny spots (6)
To give a first or Christian name to (7)
To receive from one who has gone before (7)
Uncontrolled laughing or crying (10)
Walked in a heavy-footed way; plodded (7)
Walked in a pompous way; swaggered (8)
Weak; without much energy (6)
Went down (9)
White, fluffy clouds with a flat base (7)
Wooden, xylophone-like instruments (8)

House on Mango Street Vocabulary Word Search 1 Answer Key

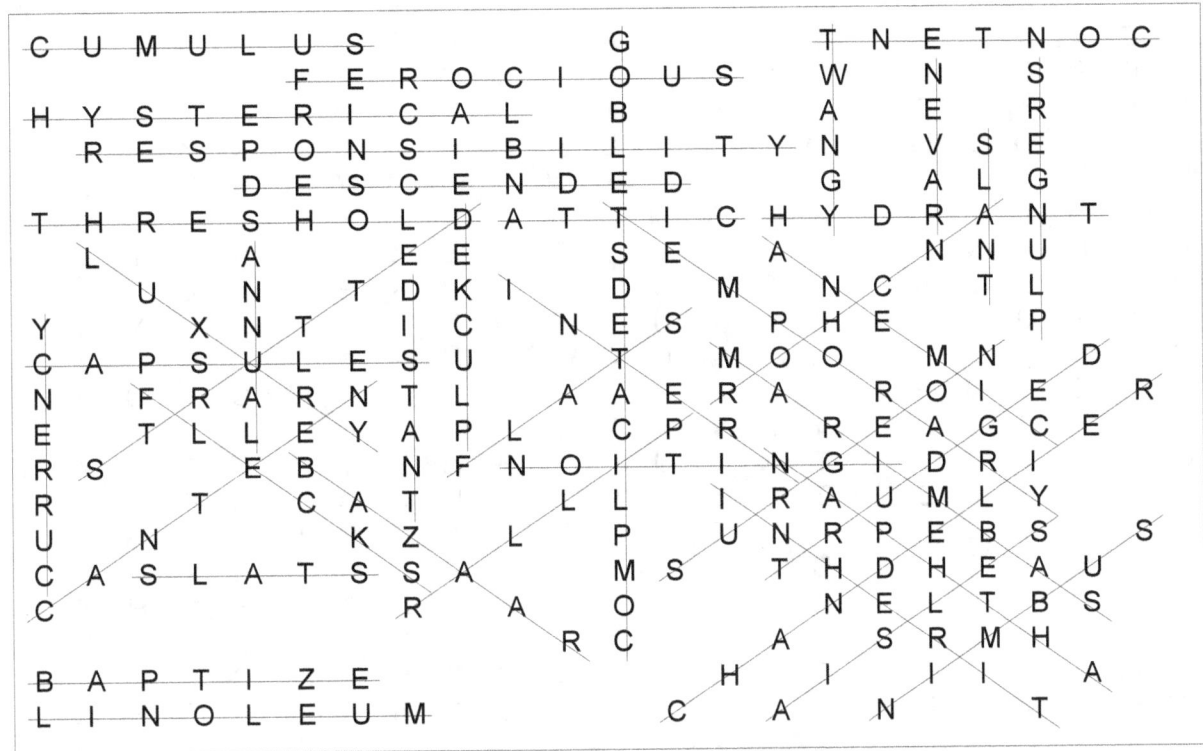

A column or vertical support (6)
A doctor who operates on patients (7)
A fair or sale (6)
A kind of soap (7)
A large bird with black feathers (5)
A light fixture that hangs from a ceiling (10)
A low, dark rain cloud (6)
A room directly below the roof (5)
A sharp, vibrating sound (6)
A small cafeteria or snack bar (7)
A washable floor covering (8)
An advanced student (6)
An entrance or doorway (9)
An upright cylinder for holding water (7)
Apartments all on one floor (5)
Comfort and pleasure (6)
Done every year (6)
Duty (14)
Far apart in relationship (7)
For a limited time (9)
Glasses with stems and bases (7)
Heavy object used to keep a boat in place (6)
Money (8)

Narrow strips of wood or metal (5)
Not easy to understand (11)
Passageways in a store or theater (6)
Removed with the fingers (7)
Rubber suction cups on sticks (8)
Satisfied (7)
Savage, fierce (9)
Slope; go in a diagonal direction (5)
Small, oval shaped, jelly-like container (8)
The switch that turns on a car (8)
Tiny spots (6)
To give a first or Christian name to (7)
To receive from one who has gone before (7)
Uncontrolled laughing or crying (10)
Walked in a heavy-footed way; plodded (7)
Walked in a pompous way; swaggered (8)
Weak; without much energy (6)
Went down (9)
White, fluffy clouds with a flat base (7)
Wooden, xylophone-like instruments (8)

House on Mango Street Vocabulary Word Search 2

```
F G T N A R D Y H I G N I T I O N S B M L T
J E R D D U Q M Q P R C E Q Q N U X U H A R
A A R Z E D T F A E L M A P K B H E V J C F
N T S O S Q L O T R P U K N M P L E R Z I X
N T T C C D R N M O I Z N I T O V K R W R L
U I R A E I I X R A M M N G N E H R T I E M
A C U P N Y O A S Q T S B I E Z E N K P T M
L F T S D S R U S W S I L A H R E N R L S F
W X T U E Y L K S T U H C D S T S A X U Y V
M L E L D D C A A M L C B A N N A G Q C H Y
D M D E Q E F L N F U O T O L Z B G C K Q P
L D K S L L F V R T M M C S A L B W T E Y D
O T J F G S D T N S U P Y B N Z Y T D D T Y
H V S W T E H Z U N C L Z F D B C I A W C S
S M S M G K P R W E Z I T P A B S I B N G C
E G Q D T I G D N N F C S W Z T S B E P I M
R G U N L E H J E X V A L F A L C R B M H X
H R V L O Q T V W C M T A N E Q R D E K S N
T W A N G Y A G O B L E T S P U A N C H O R
W R K W Y R U X U L M D S G C N A P H T H A
```

A column or vertical support (6)
A doctor who operates on patients (7)
A fair or sale (6)
A kind of soap (7)
A large bird with black feathers (5)
A low, dark rain cloud (6)
A room directly below the roof (5)
A sharp, vibrating sound (6)
A small cafeteria or snack bar (7)
A washable floor covering (8)
An advanced student (6)
An entrance or doorway (9)
An upright cylinder for holding water (7)
Apartments all on one floor (5)
Comfort and pleasure (6)
Done by machine (13)
Done every year (6)
Far apart in relationship (7)
For a limited time (9)
Glasses with stems and bases (7)
Heavy object used to keep a boat in place (6)
Money (8)
Narrow strips of wood or metal (5)

Not easy to understand (11)
Passageways in a store or theater (6)
Removed with the fingers (7)
Rubber suction cups on sticks (8)
Satisfied (7)
Savage, fierce (9)
Slope; go in a diagonal direction (5)
Small, oval shaped, jelly-like container (8)
The switch that turns on a car (8)
Tiny spots (6)
To give a first or Christian name to (7)
To receive from one who has gone before (7)
Uncontrolled laughing or crying (10)
Walked in a heavy-footed way; plodded (7)
Walked in a pompous way; swaggered (8)
Weak; without much energy (6)
Went down (9)
White, fluffy clouds with a flat base (7)
Wooden, xylophone-like instruments (8)

House on Mango Street Vocabulary Word Search 2 Answer Key

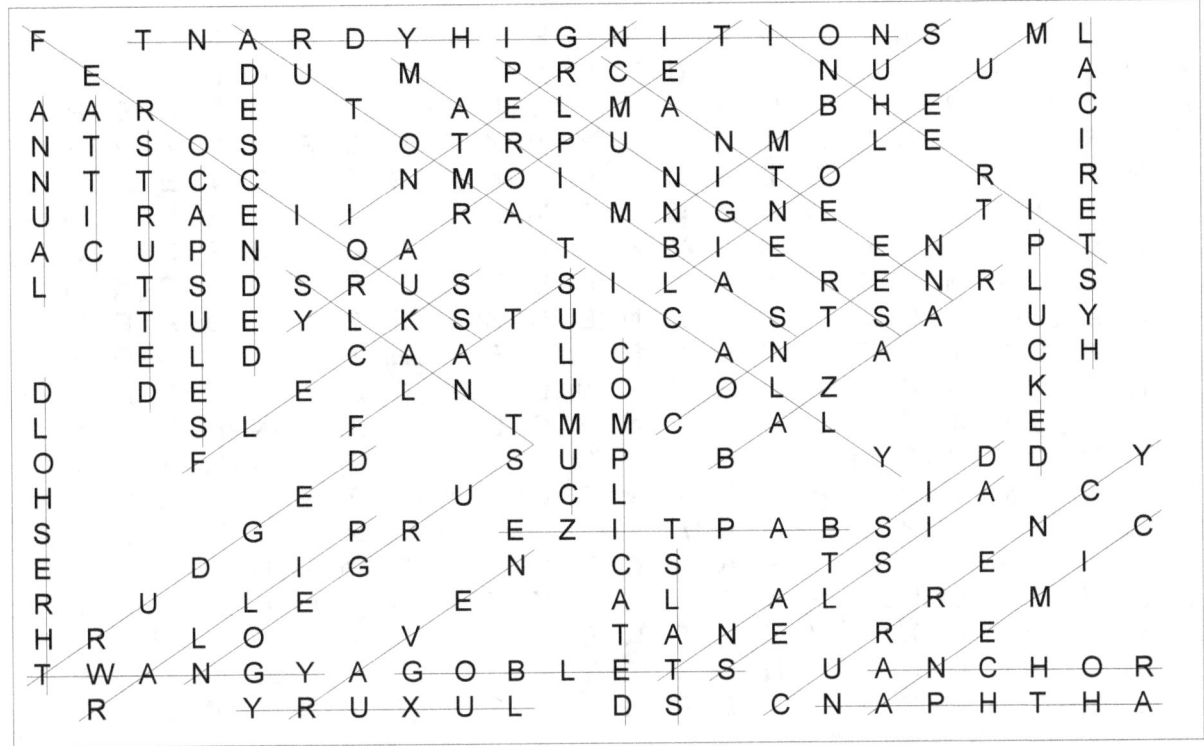

A column or vertical support (6)
A doctor who operates on patients (7)
A fair or sale (6)
A kind of soap (7)
A large bird with black feathers (5)
A low, dark rain cloud (6)
A room directly below the roof (5)
A sharp, vibrating sound (6)
A small cafeteria or snack bar (7)
A washable floor covering (8)
An advanced student (6)
An entrance or doorway (9)
An upright cylinder for holding water (7)
Apartments all on one floor (5)
Comfort and pleasure (6)
Done by machine (13)
Done every year (6)
Far apart in relationship (7)
For a limited time (9)
Glasses with stems and bases (7)
Heavy object used to keep a boat in place (6)
Money (8)
Narrow strips of wood or metal (5)
Not easy to understand (11)
Passageways in a store or theater (6)
Removed with the fingers (7)
Rubber suction cups on sticks (8)
Satisfied (7)
Savage, fierce (9)
Slope; go in a diagonal direction (5)
Small, oval shaped, jelly-like container (8)
The switch that turns on a car (8)
Tiny spots (6)
To give a first or Christian name to (7)
To receive from one who has gone before (7)
Uncontrolled laughing or crying (10)
Walked in a heavy-footed way; plodded (7)
Walked in a pompous way; swaggered (8)
Weak; without much energy (6)
Went down (9)
White, fluffy clouds with a flat base (7)
Wooden, xylophone-like instruments (8)

House on Mango Street Vocabulary Word Search 1

```
B H P F V P W F F L X F S T H R E S H O L D H P S
A Q K J V H M L E F A U T O M A T I C A L L Y K J
P Y X D D R N Y L R N Y T I L I B I S N O P S E R
T F R Y T T O M Z K O Y D Y N Z S L Q F F H T P S
I P H Y Y M I D E T A C I L P M O C F M Q J E L D
Z S Y B J J T Y Q C J Q I R W B Z U A R B R R U M
E L D Y T L I K J M H Y S O A H Z R D P O P I C G
X N R F A H N Q R T Z A P D U V D R D H S L C K G
J J A U G P G H J J M N N E N S E E C L Y U A E Y
Y G N A W T I T R U D G E D O B I N T E R N L D R
T N T I Y T C L E X R C A N E T A C Z A U G S E B
A S J X M J E L L Q Z I N E G L J Y A D X E L T S
S E M M H B O M K A C T E C R G I Z L I U R A T T
F L A T S N U W P S R T M S U O A E F S L S N U Z
X S R F I P H S U O I A I E S B H G R T L T T R K
Y I I L R S K L D R R L C D H L T F W A H A F T C
D A M K Z S U W E K T A X H K E H Q P N S J T S S
C V B G S M X H N Q W F R B T T P Q J T W F W S C
V W A F U Q N H K N X M T Y Y S A F L E C K S D V
Y L S C K I C A N T E E N K C O N T E N T M S G W
```

AISLES	DESCENDED	NIMBUS
ANCHOR	DISTANT	PILLAR
ANEMIC	FEROCIOUS	PLUCKED
ANNUAL	FLATS	PLUNGERS
ATTIC	FLECKS	RAVEN
AUTOMATICALLY	GOBLETS	RESPONSIBILITY
BAPTIZE	HYDRANT	SLANT
BAZAAR	HYSTERICAL	SLATS
CANTEEN	IGNITION	STRUTTED
CAPSULES	INHERIT	SURGEON
CHANDELIER	INTERN	TEMPORARY
COMPLICATED	LINOLEUM	THRESHOLD
CONTENT	LUXURY	TRUDGED
CUMULUS	MARIMBAS	TWANGY
CURRENCY	NAPHTHA	

House on Mango Street Vocabulary Word Search 3 Answer Key

AISLES	DESCENDED	NIMBUS
ANCHOR	DISTANT	PILLAR
ANEMIC	FEROCIOUS	PLUCKED
ANNUAL	FLATS	PLUNGERS
ATTIC	FLECKS	RAVEN
AUTOMATICALLY	GOBLETS	RESPONSIBILITY
BAPTIZE	HYDRANT	SLANT
BAZAAR	HYSTERICAL	SLATS
CANTEEN	IGNITION	STRUTTED
CAPSULES	INHERIT	SURGEON
CHANDELIER	INTERN	TEMPORARY
COMPLICATED	LINOLEUM	THRESHOLD
CONTENT	LUXURY	TRUDGED
CUMULUS	MARIMBAS	TWANGY
CURRENCY	NAPHTHA	

House on Mango Street Vocabulary Crossword 4

```
F R Q K H V H N K R N T C O M P L I C A T E D S D
E E D S G N O N N O K E L T Z F E A Q F B X Q G E
R S L M B E C Y I L R M D Y Y Z Z K N W L B B G D
O P Y F G Z P T F S R P W J I Y S K X N F E H B N
C O Y R J P I N B A R O N T W H S T R T U X C J E
I N U P W N P A L B C R P L T A K G R R S A C K C
O S R E G N U L P R A A Z A B S H O C U M U L U S
U I L I R J I S U G B R N M T G Y B M D T G F E E
S B H A T P A H D X H Y I T N S D L F G Z T L D D
I I T Y T H N N P S U R F T E G R E T E T U E R T
N L N L S S R A E H A R K L V E A T L D S C O D B
T I A H I T Y E P M V I Y R A B N S R P I H F N K
E T T B E N E S S H I J S P R T T W A T C A S Q D
R Y S X T R O R Z H T C J L L S S C T N U N T P M
N V I V W S I L I R O H W U E T R A A W R D P J P
G P D C A M D T E C X L A C V S Z W L N R E K X D
T N E T N O C T P U A J D K N I M B U S E L V W H
S G L B G S Z F L V M L T E M T Y L Q P N I F F Z
W H B T Y D R Z L Q V P K D Q Z F C D D C E F F Y
A U T O M A T I C A L L Y X C Q K H R M Y R N M S
```

AISLES
ANCHOR
ANEMIC
ANNUAL
ATTIC
AUTOMATICALLY
BAPTIZE
BAZAAR
CANTEEN
CAPSULES
CHANDELIER
COMPLICATED
CONTENT
CUMULUS
CURRENCY

DESCENDED
DISTANT
FEROCIOUS
FLATS
FLECKS
GOBLETS
HYDRANT
HYSTERICAL
IGNITION
INHERIT
INTERN
LINOLEUM
LUXURY
MARIMBAS
NAPHTHA

NIMBUS
PILLAR
PLUCKED
PLUNGERS
RAVEN
RESPONSIBILITY
SLANT
SLATS
STRUTTED
SURGEON
TEMPORARY
THRESHOLD
TRUDGED
TWANGY

House on Mango Street Vocabulary Crssword 4 Answer Key

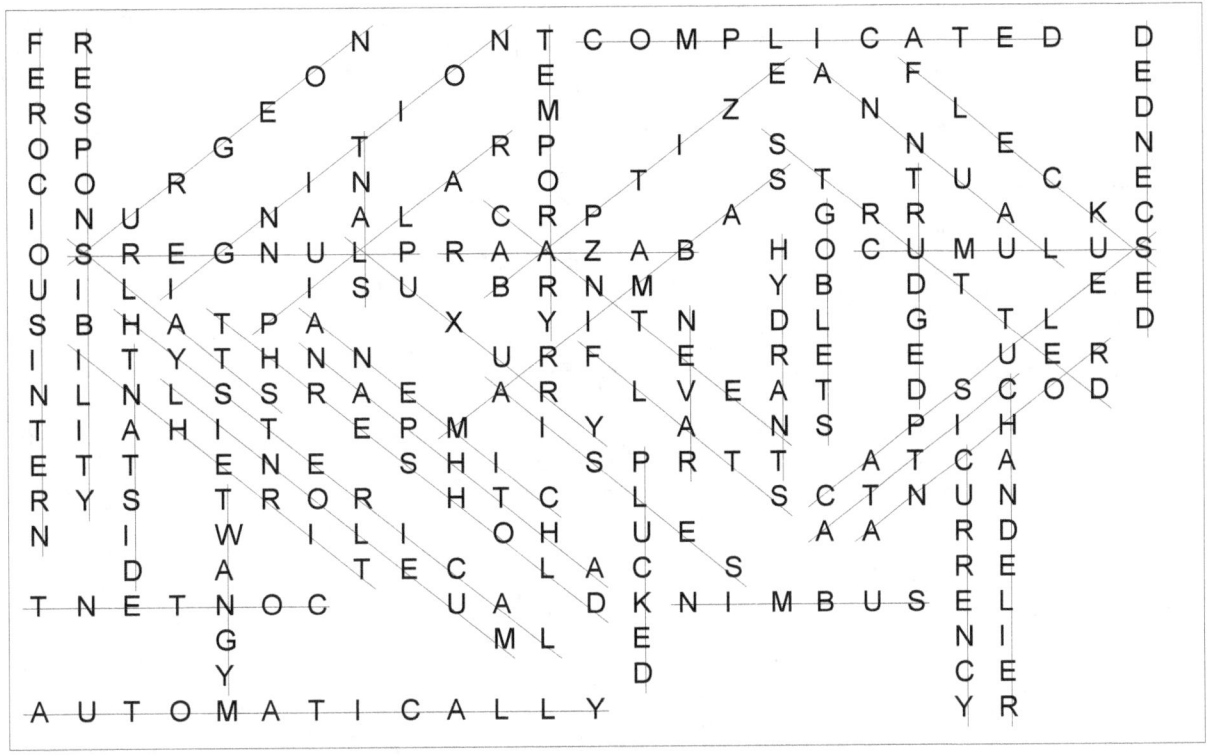

AISLES	DESCENDED	NIMBUS
ANCHOR	DISTANT	PILLAR
ANEMIC	FEROCIOUS	PLUCKED
ANNUAL	FLATS	PLUNGERS
ATTIC	FLECKS	RAVEN
AUTOMATICALLY	GOBLETS	RESPONSIBILITY
BAPTIZE	HYDRANT	SLANT
BAZAAR	HYSTERICAL	SLATS
CANTEEN	IGNITION	STRUTTED
CAPSULES	INHERIT	SURGEON
CHANDELIER	INTERN	TEMPORARY
COMPLICATED	LINOLEUM	THRESHOLD
CONTENT	LUXURY	TRUDGED
CUMULUS	MARIMBAS	TWANGY
CURRENCY	NAPHTHA	

House On Mango Street Vocabulary Crossword 1

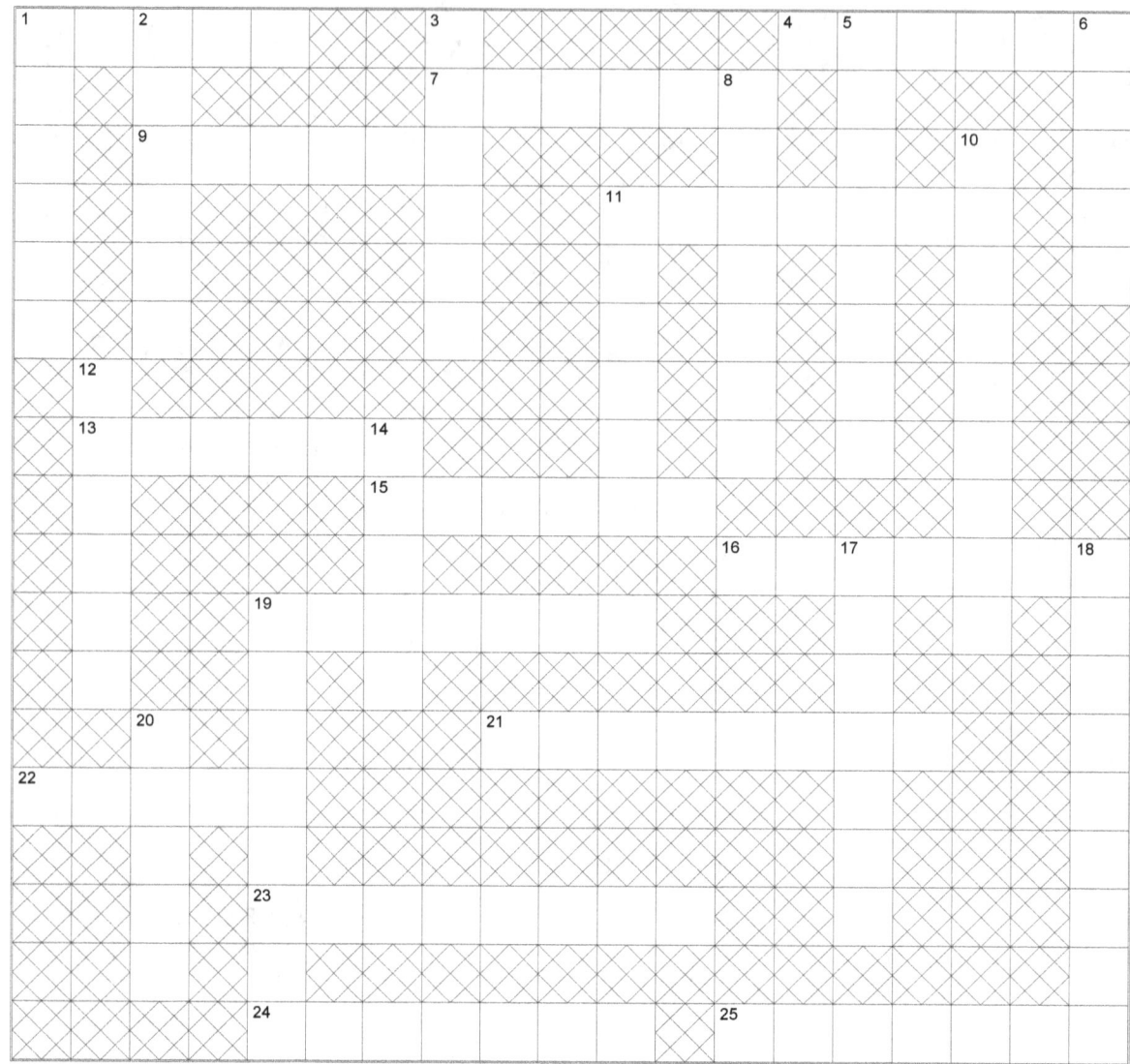

Across
1. A room directly below the roof
4. Passageways in a store or theater
7. An advanced student
9. Done every year
11. To give a first or Christian name to
13. A low, dark rain cloud
15. Comfort and pleasure
16. To receive from one who has gone before
19. Satisfied
21. Rubber suction cups on sticks
22. Apartments all on one floor
23. A washable floor covering
24. A doctor who operates on patients
25. Removed with the fingers

Down
1. Heavy object used to keep a boat in place
2. A sharp, vibrating sound
3. A column or vertical support
5. The switch that turns on a car
6. Narrow strips of wood or metal
8. A kind of soap
10. For a limited time
11. A fair or sale
12. Weak; without much energy
14. Slope; go in a diagonal direction
17. An upright cylinder for holding water
18. An entrance or doorway
19. Small, oval shaped, jelly-like container
20. A large bird with black feathers

House On Mango Street Vocabulary Crossword 1 Answer Key

	1	2	3	4	5	6	7	8	9	10	11	12	13
1	A	T	T	I	C		3P			4A	5I	S	L	E	6S

Grid answers:
- 1A ATTIC
- 4A AISLES
- 7A INTERN
- 9A ANNUAL
- 11A BAPTIZE
- 13A NIMBUS
- 15A LUXURY
- 16A INHERIT
- 19A CONTENT
- 21A PLUNGERS
- 22A FLATS
- 23A LINOLEUM
- 24A SURGEON
- 25A PLUCKED

- 1D ANCHOR
- 2D TWANGY
- 3D PILLAR
- 5D IGNITION
- 6D SLATS
- 8D NAPHTHA
- 10D TEMPORARY
- 11D BAZAAR
- 12D ANEMIC
- 14D SLANT
- 17D HYDRANT
- 18D THRESHOLD
- 19D CAPSULE
- 20D RAVEN

Across
1. A room directly below the roof
4. Passageways in a store or theater
7. An advanced student
9. Done every year
11. To give a first or Christian name to
13. A low, dark rain cloud
15. Comfort and pleasure
16. To receive from one who has gone before
19. Satisfied
21. Rubber suction cups on sticks
22. Apartments all on one floor
23. A washable floor covering
24. A doctor who operates on patients
25. Removed with the fingers

Down
1. Heavy object used to keep a boat in place
2. A sharp, vibrating sound
3. A column or vertical support
5. The switch that turns on a car
6. Narrow strips of wood or metal
8. A kind of soap
10. For a limited time
11. A fair or sale
12. Weak; without much energy
14. Slope; go in a diagonal direction
17. An upright cylinder for holding water
18. An entrance or doorway
19. Small, oval shaped, jelly-like container
20. A large bird with black feathers

House On Mango Street Vocabulary Crossword 2

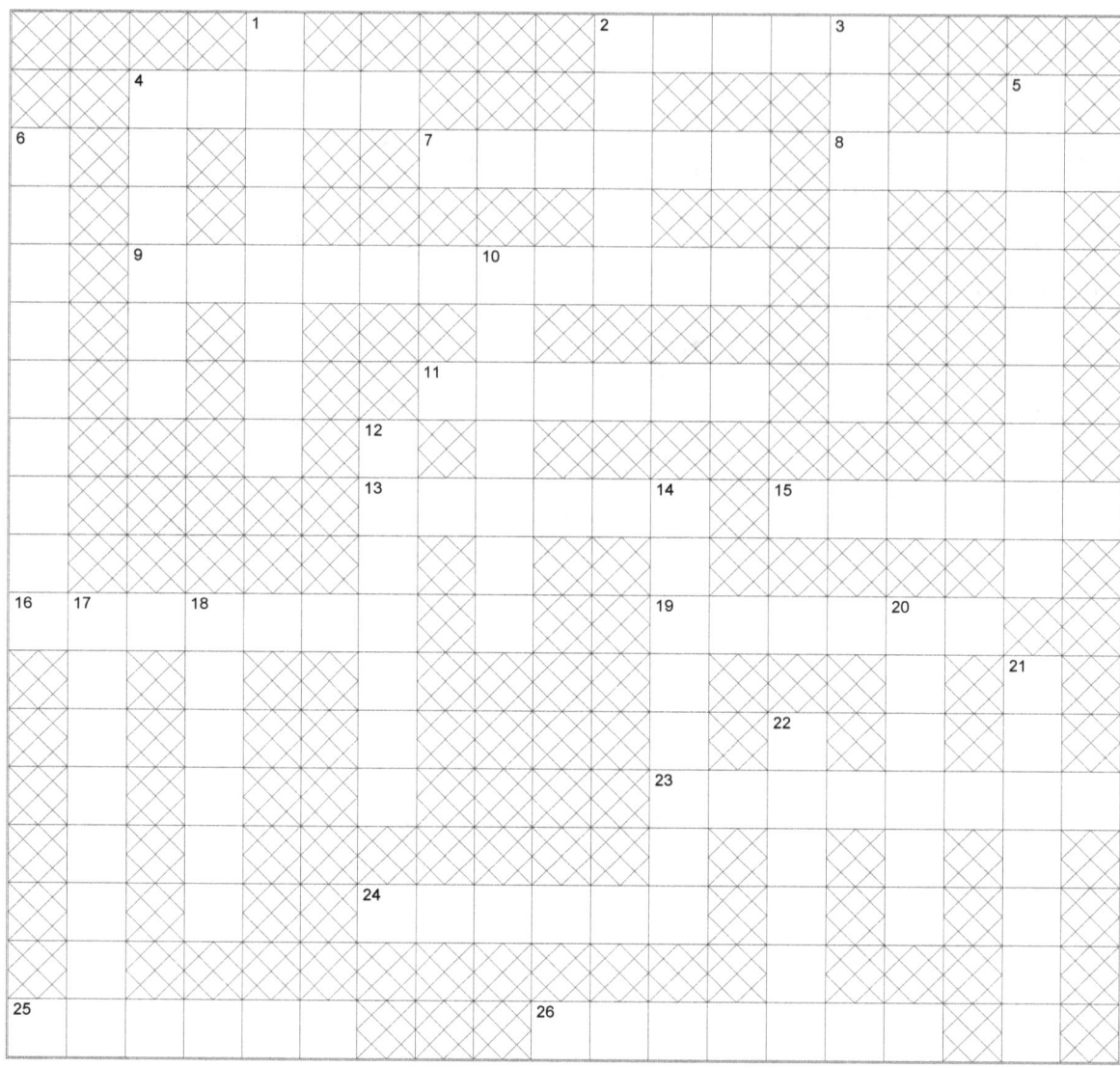

Across
2. Narrow strips of wood or metal
4. Apartments all on one floor
7. A fair or sale
8. A large bird with black feathers
9. Not easy to understand
11. An advanced student
13. Weak; without much energy
15. Comfort and pleasure
16. Far apart in relationship
19. A column or vertical support
23. A washable floor covering
24. A low, dark rain cloud
25. Heavy object used to keep a boat in place
26. White, fluffy clouds with a flat base

Down
1. Wooden, xylophone-like instruments
2. Slope; go in a diagonal direction
3. A doctor who operates on patients
4. Tiny spots
5. For a limited time
6. An entrance or doorway
10. Satisfied
12. To give a first or Christian name to
14. Small, oval shaped, jelly-like container
17. The switch that turns on a car
18. A sharp, vibrating sound
20. Passageways in a store or theater
21. Removed with the fingers
22. Done every year

House On Mango Street Vocabulary Crossword 2 Answer Key

			1 M				2 S	L	A	T	S	3 S				
		4 F	L	A	T	S					L		U		5 T	
6 T		L		R		7 B	A	Z	A	A	R		8 R	A	V	E	N
H		E		I					N				G		M	
R	9	C	O	M	P	L	I	10 C	A	T	E	D		E		P
E		K		B				O					E		O
S		S		A		11	I	N	T	E	R	N			O
H				S		12 B		T							R
O						13 A	N	E	M	I	14 C		15 L	U	X	U	R	Y
L						P		N			A				Y
16 D	17 I	18 S	T	A	N	T				19 P	I	L	L	20 A	R
	G		W			I				S				I		21 P
	N		A			Z				U	22 A		S		L
	I		N			E			23 L	I	N	O	L	E	U	M
	T		G						E		N		E		C
	I		Y		24 N	I	M	B	U	S		U		S		K
	O								A			E				E
25 A	N	C	H	O	R		26 C	U	M	U	L	U	S		D

Across
2. Narrow strips of wood or metal
4. Apartments all on one floor
7. A fair or sale
8. A large bird with black feathers
9. Not easy to understand
11. An advanced student
13. Weak; without much energy
15. Comfort and pleasure
16. Far apart in relationship
19. A column or vertical support
23. A washable floor covering
24. A low, dark rain cloud
25. Heavy object used to keep a boat in place
26. White, fluffy clouds with a flat base

Down
1. Wooden, xylophone-like instruments
2. Slope; go in a diagonal direction
3. A doctor who operates on patients
4. Tiny spots
5. For a limited time
6. An entrance or doorway
10. Satisfied
12. To give a first or Christian name to
14. Small, oval shaped, jelly-like container
17. The switch that turns on a car
18. A sharp, vibrating sound
20. Passageways in a store or theater
21. Removed with the fingers
22. Done every year

House On Mango Street Vocabulary Crossword 3

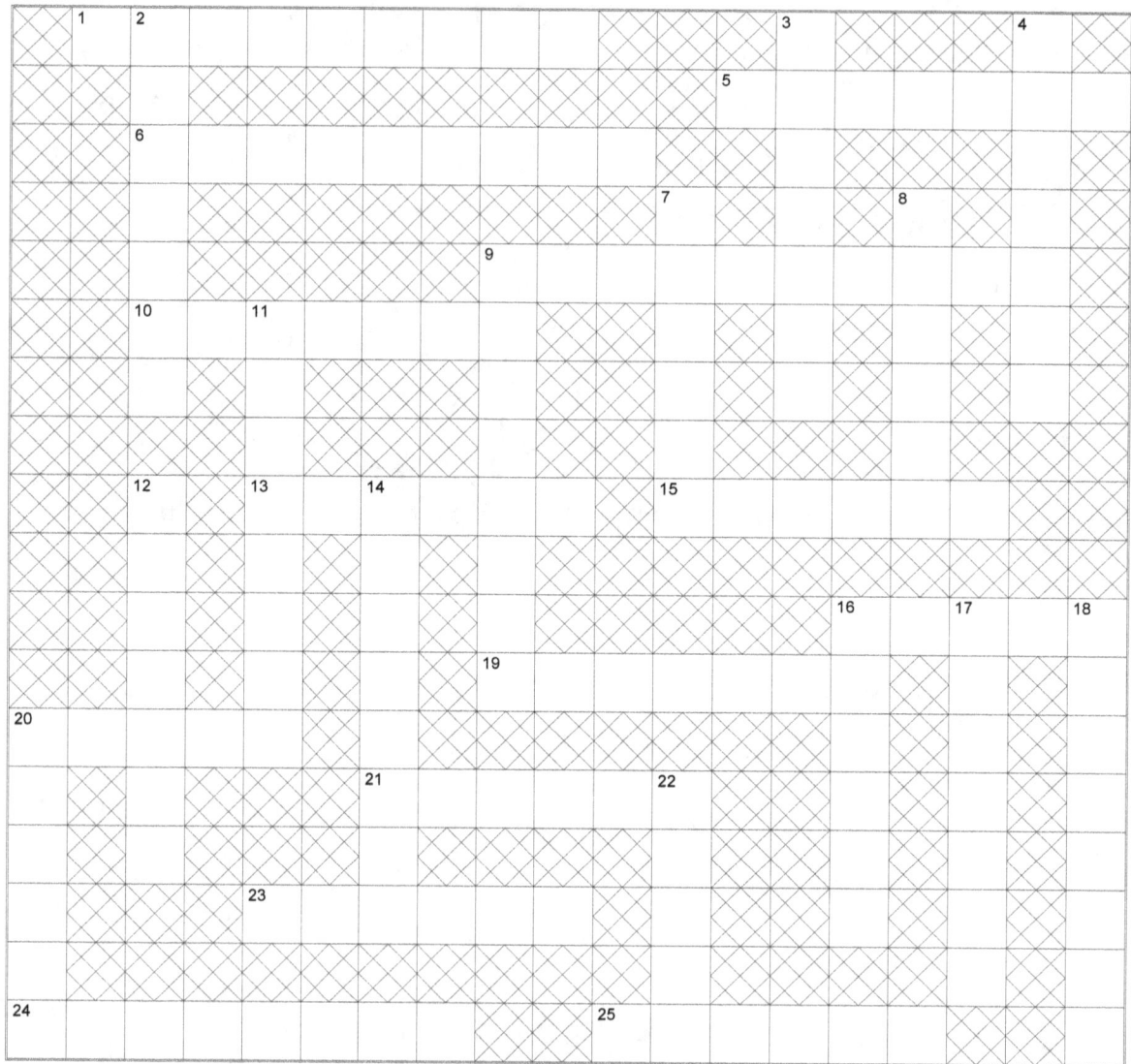

Across
1. An entrance or doorway
5. Satisfied
6. Went down
9. A light fixture that hangs from a ceiling
10. A kind of soap
13. A low, dark rain cloud
15. Comfort and pleasure
16. A room directly below the roof
19. A doctor who operates on patients
20. Apartments all on one floor
21. A fair or sale
23. Passageways in a store or theater
24. Walked in a pompous way; swaggered
25. Heavy object used to keep a boat in place

Down
2. An upright cylinder for holding water
3. Glasses with stems and bases
4. To receive from one who has gone before
7. Done every year
8. A column or vertical support
9. Small, oval shaped, jelly-like container
11. Rubber suction cups on sticks
12. Far apart in relationship
14. Wooden, xylophone-like instruments
16. Weak; without much energy
17. Walked in a heavy-footed way; plodded
18. Money
20. Tiny spots
22. A large bird with black feathers

House On Mango Street Vocabulary Crossword 3 Answer Key

	1	2							3			4	
	T	H	R	E	S	H	O	L	D			I	
		Y						5	C	O	N	T	E N T
		6 D	E	S	C	E	N	D	E D		B		H
		R					7 A		L	8 P		E
		A			9 C	H	A	N	D	E	L	I	E R
		10 N	11 A	P	H	T	H	A		N	T	L	I
		T	L					P		U	S	L	T
			U					S		A		A	
		12 D	13 N	I	14 M	B	U	S		15 L	U	X U R Y
		I	G		A			L				16 A	17 T	18 C
		S	E		R			E				T T I C
		T	R		I		19 S	U	R	G	E	O N R U
20 F	L	A	T	S		M						E U R
L		N		21 B	A	Z	A	A	22 R			M D R
E		T			A				A			I G E
C			23 A	I	S	L	E	S	V			C E N
K									E			D C
24 S	T	R	U	T	T	E	D		25 A	N	C	H O R Y

Across
1. An entrance or doorway
5. Satisfied
6. Went down
9. A light fixture that hangs from a ceiling
10. A kind of soap
13. A low, dark rain cloud
15. Comfort and pleasure
16. A room directly below the roof
19. A doctor who operates on patients
20. Apartments all on one floor
21. A fair or sale
23. Passageways in a store or theater
24. Walked in a pompous way; swaggered
25. Heavy object used to keep a boat in place

Down
2. An upright cylinder for holding water
3. Glasses with stems and bases
4. To receive from one who has gone before
7. Done every year
8. A column or vertical support
9. Small, oval shaped, jelly-like container
11. Rubber suction cups on sticks
12. Far apart in relationship
14. Wooden, xylophone-like instruments
16. Weak; without much energy
17. Walked in a heavy-footed way; plodded
18. Money
20. Tiny spots
22. A large bird with black feathers

House On Mango Street Vocabulary Crossword 4

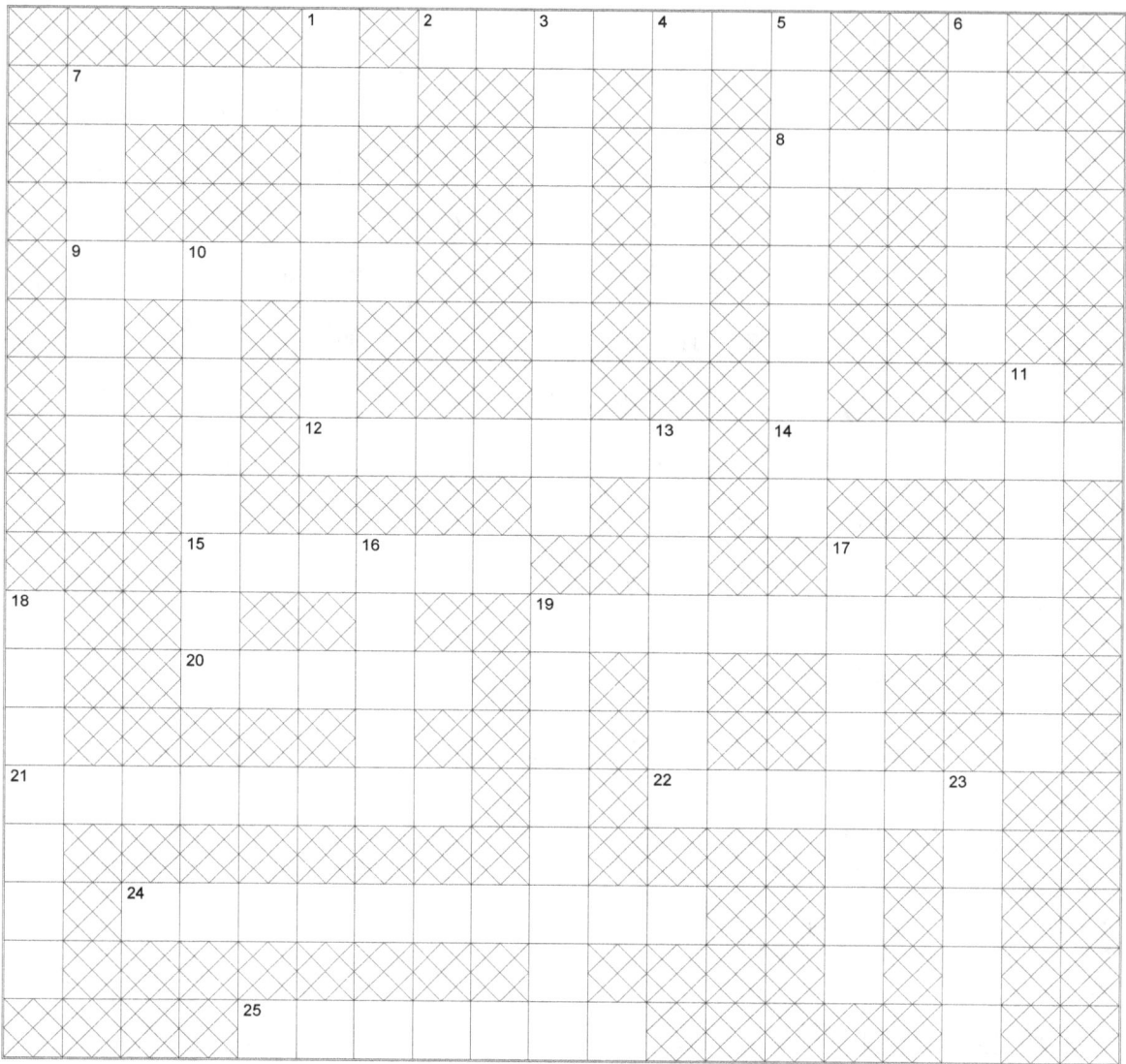

Across
2. An upright cylinder for holding water
7. A column or vertical support
8. A large bird with black feathers
9. A low, dark rain cloud
12. A doctor who operates on patients
14. Comfort and pleasure
15. A fair or sale
19. To receive from one who has gone before
20. Narrow strips of wood or metal
21. Money
22. Passageways in a store or theater
24. A light fixture that hangs from a ceiling
25. Satisfied

Down
1. Small, oval shaped, jelly-like container
3. Went down
4. Done every year
5. An entrance or doorway
6. Weak; without much energy
7. Rubber suction cups on sticks
10. Wooden, xylophone-like instruments
11. Walked in a heavy-footed way; plodded
13. A kind of soap
16. A room directly below the roof
17. A washable floor covering
18. Removed with the fingers
19. The switch that turns on a car
23. Slope; go in a diagonal direction

House On Mango Street Vocabulary Crossword 4 Answer Key

			1 C		2 H	Y	3 D	R	4 A	N	5 T		6 A	
	7 P	I	L	L	A	R		E		N		H		N
	L				P			S		N	8 R	A	V	E	N
	U				S			C		U		E		M
	9 N	I	10 M	B	U	S		E		A		S		I
	G		A		L			N		L		H		C
	E		R		E			D				O		11 T
	R		I		12 S	U	R	G	E	13 O	N	14 L	U	X	U	R	Y
	S		M					D		A		D		U
			15 B	A	16 Z	A	A	R		P		17 L		D
18 P			A		T			19 I	N	H	E	R	I	T	G
L			20 S	L	A	T	S		G		T		N		E
U					I				N		H		O		D
21 C	U	R	R	E	N	C	Y		22 I		A	I	S	L	E	23 S
K									T				E		L
E		24 C	H	A	N	D	E	L	I	E	R		U		A
D									O				M		N
		25 C	O	N	T	E	N	T						T

Across

2. An upright cylinder for holding water
7. A column or vertical support
8. A large bird with black feathers
9. A low, dark rain cloud
12. A doctor who operates on patients
14. Comfort and pleasure
15. A fair or sale
19. To receive from one who has gone before
20. Narrow strips of wood or metal
21. Money
22. Passageways in a store or theater
24. A light fixture that hangs from a ceiling
25. Satisfied

Down

1. Small, oval shaped, jelly-like container
3. Went down
4. Done every year
5. An entrance or doorway
6. Weak; without much energy
7. Rubber suction cups on sticks
10. Wooden, xylophone-like instruments
11. Walked in a heavy-footed way; plodded
13. A kind of soap
16. A room directly below the roof
17. A washable floor covering
18. Removed with the fingers
19. The switch that turns on a car
23. Slope; go in a diagonal direction

House on Mango Street Vocabulary Juggle Letters 1

1. MICANE = 1. _____
Weak; without much energy

2. MECILOPDTCA = 2. _____
Not easy to understand

3. TLNSA = 3. _____
Slope; go in a diagonal direction

4. NANTEEC = 4. _____
A small cafeteria or snack bar

5. TAAHPNH = 5. _____
A kind of soap

6. SHOERLDTH = 6. _____
An entrance or doorway

7. DTURSTET = 7. _____
Walked in a pompous way; swaggered

8. EURDGDT = 8. _____
Walked in a heavy-footed way; plodded

9. LPAUSCSE = 9. _____
Small, oval shaped, jelly-like container

10. YNAWTG =10. _____
A sharp, vibrating sound

11. BSLTGOE =11. _____
Glasses with stems and bases

12. NCCREYRU =12. _____
Money

13. KFLECS =13. _____
Tiny spots

14. LMCSUUU =14. _____
White, fluffy clouds with a flat base

15. SLTAF =15. _____
Apartments all on one floor

House on Mango Street Vocabulary Juggle Letters 1 Answer Key

1. MICANE = 1. ANEMIC
   Weak; without much energy

2. MECILOPDTCA = 2. COMPLICATED
   Not easy to understand

3. TLNSA = 3. SLANT
   Slope; go in a diagonal direction

4. NANTEEC = 4. CANTEEN
   A small cafeteria or snack bar

5. TAAHPNH = 5. NAPHTHA
   A kind of soap

6. SHOERLDTH = 6. THRESHOLD
   An entrance or doorway

7. DTURSTET = 7. STRUTTED
   Walked in a pompous way; swaggered

8. EURDGDT = 8. TRUDGED
   Walked in a heavy-footed way; plodded

9. LPAUSCSE = 9. CAPSULES
   Small, oval shaped, jelly-like container

10. YNAWTG = 10. TWANGY
    A sharp, vibrating sound

11. BSLTGOE = 11. GOBLETS
    Glasses with stems and bases

12. NCCREYRU = 12. CURRENCY
    Money

13. KFLECS = 13. FLECKS
    Tiny spots

14. LMCSUUU = 14. CUMULUS
    White, fluffy clouds with a flat base

15. SLTAF = 15. FLATS
    Apartments all on one floor

House on Mango Street Vocabulary Juggle Letters 2

1. EADCILMOTPC = 1. _____
   Not easy to understand

2. RETAROPMY = 2. _____
   For a limited time

3. SBNIMU = 3. _____
   A low, dark rain cloud

4. NDITATS = 4. _____
   Far apart in relationship

5. URXYUL = 5. _____
   Comfort and pleasure

6. RTENNI = 6. _____
   An advanced student

7. SONEGUR = 7. _____
   A doctor who operates on patients

8. EANRV = 8. _____
   A large bird with black feathers

9. NANLAU = 9. _____
   Done every year

10. TRADNYH = 10. _____
    An upright cylinder for holding water

11. IIINTGON = 11. _____
    The switch that turns on a car

12. DERICAHLNE = 12. _____
    A light fixture that hangs from a ceiling

13. NNTACEE = 13. _____
    A small cafeteria or snack bar

14. ENILULMO = 14. _____
    A washable floor covering

15. MULUSUC = 15. _____
    White, fluffy clouds with a flat base

House on Mango Street Vocabulary Juggle Letters 2 Answer Key

1. EADCILMOTPC = 1. COMPLICATED
Not easy to understand

2. RETAROPMY = 2. TEMPORARY
For a limited time

3. SBNIMU = 3. NIMBUS
A low, dark rain cloud

4. NDITATS = 4. DISTANT
Far apart in relationship

5. URXYUL = 5. LUXURY
Comfort and pleasure

6. RTENNI = 6. INTERN
An advanced student

7. SONEGUR = 7. SURGEON
A doctor who operates on patients

8. EANRV = 8. RAVEN
A large bird with black feathers

9. NANLAU = 9. ANNUAL
Done every year

10. TRADNYH = 10. HYDRANT
An upright cylinder for holding water

11. IIINTGON = 11. IGNITION
The switch that turns on a car

12. DERICAHLNE = 12. CHANDELIER
A light fixture that hangs from a ceiling

13. NNTACEE = 13. CANTEEN
A small cafeteria or snack bar

14. ENILULMO = 14. LINOLEUM
A washable floor covering

15. MULUSUC = 15. CUMULUS
White, fluffy clouds with a flat base

House on Mango Street Vocabulary Juggle Letters 3

1. DEDECDSEN = 1. _____
   Went down

2. LEASSI = 2. _____
   Passageways in a store or theater

3. NTYHADR = 3. _____
   An upright cylinder for holding water

4. SUMNIB = 4. _____
   A low, dark rain cloud

5. IDSNATT = 5. _____
   Far apart in relationship

6. EPTOYRRAM = 6. _____
   For a limited time

7. AYLTCOALTMIAU = 7. _____
   Done by machine

8. AZAARB = 8. _____
   A fair or sale

9. ETINIORPSBSYIL = 9. _____
   Duty

10. EITRNN =10. _____
    An advanced student

11. LETODHRSH =11. _____
    An entrance or doorway

12. REIDAENLCH =12. _____
    A light fixture that hangs from a ceiling

13. TNTNOEC =13. _____
    Satisfied

14. ERAVN =14. _____
    A large bird with black feathers

15. AWNGYT =15. _____
    A sharp, vibrating sound

House on Mango Street Vocabulary Crossword 3 Answer Key

1. DEDECDSEN = 1. DESCENDED
   Went down

2. LEASSI = 2. AISLES
   Passageways in a store or theater

3. NTYHADR = 3. HYDRANT
   An upright cylinder for holding water

4. SUMNIB = 4. NIMBUS
   A low, dark rain cloud

5. IDSNATT = 5. DISTANT
   Far apart in relationship

6. EPTOYRRAM = 6. TEMPORARY
   For a limited time

7. AYLTCOALTMIAU = 7. AUTOMATICALLY
   Done by machine

8. AZAARB = 8. BAZAAR
   A fair or sale

9. ETINIORPSBSYIL = 9. RESPONSIBILITY
   Duty

10. EITRNN = 10. INTERN
    An advanced student

11. LETODHRSH = 11. THRESHOLD
    An entrance or doorway

12. REIDAENLCH = 12. CHANDELIER
    A light fixture that hangs from a ceiling

13. TNTNOEC = 13. CONTENT
    Satisfied

14. ERAVN = 14. RAVEN
    A large bird with black feathers

15. AWNGYT = 15. TWANGY
    A sharp, vibrating sound

House on Mango Street Vocabulary Juggle Letters 4

1. UESOGRN = 1. _____
A doctor who operates on patients

2. AAZBAR = 2. _____
A fair or sale

3. RHCONA = 3. _____
Heavy object used to keep a boat in place

4. YTPREOMAR = 4. _____
For a limited time

5. LCSAUESP = 5. _____
Small, oval shaped, jelly-like container

6. TBZPIEA = 6. _____
To give a first or Christian name to

7. AAHNTHP = 7. _____
A kind of soap

8. BOSETLG = 8. _____
Glasses with stems and bases

9. LFCSEK = 9. _____
Tiny spots

10. ENHRTII =10. _____
To receive from one who has gone before

11. NTAITSD =11. _____
Far apart in relationship

12. TEDURGD =12. _____
Walked in a heavy-footed way; plodded

13. GAWYTN =13. _____
A sharp, vibrating sound

14. BIMARMAS =14. _____
Wooden, xylophone-like instruments

15. TICTA =15. _____
A room directly below the roof

House on Mango Street Vocabulary Juggle Letters 4 Answer Key

1. UESOGRN = 1. SURGEON
   A doctor who operates on patients

2. AAZBAR = 2. BAZAAR
   A fair or sale

3. RHCONA = 3. ANCHOR
   Heavy object used to keep a boat in place

4. YTPREOMAR = 4. TEMPORARY
   For a limited time

5. LCSAUESP = 5. CAPSULES
   Small, oval shaped, jelly-like container

6. TBZPIEA = 6. BAPTIZE
   To give a first or Christian name to

7. AAHNTHP = 7. NAPHTHA
   A kind of soap

8. BOSETLG = 8. GOBLETS
   Glasses with stems and bases

9. LFCSEK = 9. FLECKS
   Tiny spots

10. ENHRTII =10. INHERIT
    To receive from one who has gone before

11. NTAITSD =11. DISTANT
    Far apart in relationship

12. TEDURGD =12. TRUDGED
    Walked in a heavy-footed way; plodded

13. GAWYTN =13. TWANGY
    A sharp, vibrating sound

14. BIMARMAS =14. MARIMBAS
    Wooden, xylophone-like instruments

15. TICTA =15. ATTIC
    A room directly below the roof

Copyrighted

AISLES	Passageways in a store or theater
ANCHOR	Heavy object used to keep a boat in place
ANEMIC	Weak; without much energy
ANNUAL	Done every year
ATTIC	A room directly below the roof
AUTOMATICALLY	Done by machine

BAPTIZE	To give a first or Christian name to
BAZAAR	A fair or sale
CANTEEN	A small cafeteria or snack bar
CAPSULES	Small, oval shaped, jelly-like container
CHANDELIER	A light fixture that hangs from a ceiling
COMPLICATED	Not easy to understand

CONTENT	Satisfied
CUMULUS	White, fluffy clouds with a flat base
CURRENCY	Money
DESCENDED	Went down
DISTANT	Far apart in relationship
FEROCIOUS	Savage, fierce

FLATS	Apartments all on one floor
FLECKS	Tiny spots
GOBLETS	Glasses with stems and bases
HYDRANT	An upright cylinder for holding water
HYSTERICAL	Uncontrolled laughing or crying
IGNITION	The switch that turns on a car

INHERIT	To receive from one who has gone before
INTERN	An advanced student
LINOLEUM	A washable floor covering
LUXURY	Comfort and pleasure
MARIMBAS	Wooden, xylophone-like instruments
NAPHTHA	A kind of soap

NIMBUS	A low, dark rain cloud
PILLAR	A column or vertical support
PLUCKED	Removed with the fingers
PLUNGERS	Rubber suction cups on sticks
RAVEN	A large bird with black feathers
RESPONSIBILITY	Duty

SLANT	Slope; go in a diagonal direction
SLATS	Narrow strips of wood or metal
STRUTTED	Walked in a pompous way; swaggered
SURGEON	A doctor who operates on patients
TEMPORARY	For a limited time
THRESHOLD	An entrance or doorway

TRUDGED	Walked in a heavy-footed way; plodded
TWANGY	A sharp, vibrating sound

House on Mango Street Vocabulary

TEMPORARY	STRUTTED	PILLAR	THRESHOLD	IGNITION
INHERIT	SLATS	CAPSULES	CONTENT	BAZAAR
PLUNGERS	ATTIC	FREE SPACE	LUXURY	NAPHTHA
RESPONSIBILITY	FLATS	HYSTERICAL	PLUCKED	ANNUAL
CANTEEN	BAPTIZE	GOBLETS	FEROCIOUS	COMPLICATED

House on Mango Street Vocabulary

DISTANT	MARIMBAS	TRUDGED	DESCENDED	RAVEN
AISLES	CUMULUS	AUTOMATICALLY	TWANGY	NIMBUS
HYDRANT	FLECKS	FREE SPACE	CHANDELIER	INTERN
ANEMIC	CURRENCY	ANCHOR	SLANT	COMPLICATED
FEROCIOUS	GOBLETS	BAPTIZE	CANTEEN	ANNUAL

House on Mango Street Vocab

TWANGY	ANNUAL	IGNITION	HYSTERICAL	SURGEON
NAPHTHA	FLATS	SLATS	THRESHOLD	BAPTIZE
AISLES	ANEMIC	FREE SPACE	MARIMBAS	BAZAAR
GOBLETS	NIMBUS	ATTIC	DISTANT	CAPSULES
RAVEN	HYDRANT	PILLAR	TEMPORARY	STRUTTED

House on Mango Street Vocabulary

PLUCKED	LINOLEUM	CONTENT	RESPONSIBILITY	TRUDGED
FEROCIOUS	ANCHOR	CUMULUS	SLANT	AUTOMATICALLY
FLECKS	CHANDELIER	FREE SPACE	DESCENDED	INHERIT
COMPLICATED	PLUNGERS	LUXURY	CURRENCY	STRUTTED
TEMPORARY	PILLAR	HYDRANT	RAVEN	CAPSULES

House on Mango Street Vocabulary

TRUDGED	CONTENT	FEROCIOUS	BAZAAR	MARIMBAS
NIMBUS	THRESHOLD	GOBLETS	LUXURY	BAPTIZE
CAPSULES	ANCHOR	FREE SPACE	TWANGY	COMPLICATED
SLATS	RESPONSIBILITY	ATTIC	SLANT	CUMULUS
DESCENDED	LINOLEUM	FLECKS	STRUTTED	AUTOMATICALLY

House on Mango Street Vocabulary

INTERN	CHANDELIER	PLUCKED	INHERIT	FLATS
IGNITION	HYSTERICAL	CANTEEN	ANNUAL	NAPHTHA
HYDRANT	PLUNGERS	FREE SPACE	RAVEN	DISTANT
ANEMIC	AISLES	TEMPORARY	SURGEON	AUTOMATICALLY
STRUTTED	FLECKS	LINOLEUM	DESCENDED	CUMULUS

House on Mango Street Vocabulary

FLATS	THRESHOLD	NIMBUS	TRUDGED	INTERN
FEROCIOUS	ATTIC	ANEMIC	GOBLETS	PILLAR
ANCHOR	HYDRANT	FREE SPACE	TWANGY	AISLES
AUTOMATICALLY	SLANT	RESPONSIBILITY	BAPTIZE	SLATS
INHERIT	PLUCKED	BAZAAR	CAPSULES	SURGEON

House on Mango Street Vocabulary

MARIMBAS	HYSTERICAL	CONTENT	STRUTTED	CHANDELIER
DESCENDED	ANNUAL	LINOLEUM	PLUNGERS	COMPLICATED
CURRENCY	CUMULUS	FREE SPACE	TEMPORARY	FLECKS
RAVEN	NAPHTHA	LUXURY	DISTANT	SURGEON
CAPSULES	BAZAAR	PLUCKED	INHERIT	SLATS

House on Mango Street Vocabulary

SLANT	TRUDGED	ANCHOR	CONTENT	LUXURY
STRUTTED	RAVEN	CHANDELIER	INHERIT	RESPONSIBILITY
HYSTERICAL	MARIMBAS	FREE SPACE	DESCENDED	TEMPORARY
PLUNGERS	LINOLEUM	ANEMIC	TWANGY	PILLAR
ANNUAL	CAPSULES	COMPLICATED	NAPHTHA	GOBLETS

House on Mango Street Vocabulary

CUMULUS	SURGEON	HYDRANT	INTERN	FLECKS
BAZAAR	THRESHOLD	IGNITION	DISTANT	FLATS
NIMBUS	AISLES	FREE SPACE	SLATS	ATTIC
CANTEEN	FEROCIOUS	PLUCKED	AUTOMATICALLY	GOBLETS
NAPHTHA	COMPLICATED	CAPSULES	ANNUAL	PILLAR

House on Mango Street Vocabulary

COMPLICATED	BAPTIZE	HYDRANT	TEMPORARY	CANTEEN
ANCHOR	STRUTTED	PLUCKED	SURGEON	RESPONSIBILITY
IGNITION	LUXURY	FREE SPACE	CAPSULES	INTERN
RAVEN	NAPHTHA	LINOLEUM	ATTIC	PLUNGERS
SLATS	PILLAR	SLANT	AISLES	GOBLETS

House on Mango Street Vocabulary

CURRENCY	HYSTERICAL	DISTANT	CUMULUS	TWANGY
THRESHOLD	ANEMIC	INHERIT	FEROCIOUS	CONTENT
CHANDELIER	ANNUAL	FREE SPACE	BAZAAR	FLECKS
TRUDGED	AUTOMATICALLY	FLATS	NIMBUS	GOBLETS
AISLES	SLANT	PILLAR	SLATS	PLUNGERS

House on Mango Street Vocabulary

CURRENCY	FLECKS	PLUNGERS	INHERIT	ATTIC
BAZAAR	RAVEN	ANCHOR	DISTANT	AISLES
NIMBUS	CUMULUS	FREE SPACE	RESPONSIBILITY	GOBLETS
BAPTIZE	LINOLEUM	ANNUAL	FLATS	SURGEON
HYSTERICAL	SLATS	LUXURY	STRUTTED	FEROCIOUS

House on Mango Street Vocabulary

CONTENT	TRUDGED	SLANT	TEMPORARY	CANTEEN
IGNITION	NAPHTHA	PILLAR	INTERN	ANEMIC
MARIMBAS	CAPSULES	FREE SPACE	COMPLICATED	AUTOMATICALLY
HYDRANT	TWANGY	DESCENDED	THRESHOLD	FEROCIOUS
STRUTTED	LUXURY	SLATS	HYSTERICAL	SURGEON

House on Mango Street Vocabulary

TWANGY	LINOLEUM	HYSTERICAL	PLUCKED	ANNUAL
SLATS	STRUTTED	CONTENT	INTERN	RAVEN
GOBLETS	FLECKS	FREE SPACE	TEMPORARY	SURGEON
FEROCIOUS	CHANDELIER	AUTOMATICALLY	AISLES	PILLAR
ATTIC	HYDRANT	ANEMIC	CAPSULES	CANTEEN

House on Mango Street Vocabulary

BAZAAR	NIMBUS	MARIMBAS	DISTANT	FLATS
NAPHTHA	THRESHOLD	CURRENCY	LUXURY	PLUNGERS
SLANT	COMPLICATED	FREE SPACE	IGNITION	RESPONSIBILITY
BAPTIZE	CUMULUS	TRUDGED	ANCHOR	CANTEEN
CAPSULES	ANEMIC	HYDRANT	ATTIC	PILLAR

House on Mango Street Vocabulary

NIMBUS	ANCHOR	FEROCIOUS	ANEMIC	CANTEEN
STRUTTED	RESPONSIBILITY	DESCENDED	ATTIC	INHERIT
CHANDELIER	GOBLETS	FREE SPACE	TEMPORARY	HYDRANT
CAPSULES	CURRENCY	TRUDGED	PILLAR	AISLES
BAZAAR	CUMULUS	SLANT	FLECKS	LINOLEUM

House on Mango Street Vocabulary

RAVEN	PLUNGERS	NAPHTHA	ANNUAL	INTERN
SLATS	CONTENT	PLUCKED	LUXURY	DISTANT
FLATS	TWANGY	FREE SPACE	AUTOMATICALLY	SURGEON
MARIMBAS	HYSTERICAL	COMPLICATED	BAPTIZE	LINOLEUM
FLECKS	SLANT	CUMULUS	BAZAAR	AISLES

House on Mango Street Vocabulary

INHERIT	TEMPORARY	SLATS	ANEMIC	SLANT
THRESHOLD	CAPSULES	CUMULUS	COMPLICATED	NIMBUS
LINOLEUM	HYDRANT	FREE SPACE	DESCENDED	PLUNGERS
RESPONSIBILITY	NAPHTHA	MARIMBAS	FLECKS	STRUTTED
FEROCIOUS	LUXURY	TWANGY	CONTENT	PLUCKED

House on Mango Street Vocabulary

TRUDGED	ANCHOR	GOBLETS	CHANDELIER	RAVEN
CANTEEN	ANNUAL	CURRENCY	ATTIC	DISTANT
BAZAAR	FLATS	FREE SPACE	IGNITION	INTERN
AUTOMATICALLY	AISLES	HYSTERICAL	SURGEON	PLUCKED
CONTENT	TWANGY	LUXURY	FEROCIOUS	STRUTTED

House on Mango Street Vocabulary

AISLES	IGNITION	CANTEEN	PLUCKED	CUMULUS
ANCHOR	MARIMBAS	CURRENCY	HYSTERICAL	PILLAR
FLATS	NIMBUS	FREE SPACE	INHERIT	HYDRANT
TRUDGED	CONTENT	CAPSULES	ANNUAL	LINOLEUM
SURGEON	GOBLETS	AUTOMATICALLY	PLUNGERS	DISTANT

House on Mango Street Vocabulary

INTERN	SLATS	NAPHTHA	ANEMIC	DESCENDED
THRESHOLD	SLANT	TEMPORARY	CHANDELIER	LUXURY
RAVEN	FLECKS	FREE SPACE	TWANGY	RESPONSIBILITY
ATTIC	BAZAAR	FEROCIOUS	COMPLICATED	DISTANT
PLUNGERS	AUTOMATICALLY	GOBLETS	SURGEON	LINOLEUM

House on Mango Street Vocabulary

CHANDELIER	GOBLETS	RESPONSIBILITY	MARIMBAS	BAPTIZE
DISTANT	SLATS	DESCENDED	CONTENT	HYDRANT
AUTOMATICALLY	TWANGY	FREE SPACE	SURGEON	FLATS
CAPSULES	HYSTERICAL	INHERIT	NIMBUS	TRUDGED
LINOLEUM	RAVEN	PILLAR	BAZAAR	FEROCIOUS

House on Mango Street Vocabulary

ANCHOR	ANNUAL	TEMPORARY	SLANT	CUMULUS
LUXURY	THRESHOLD	AISLES	INTERN	ANEMIC
PLUCKED	STRUTTED	FREE SPACE	NAPHTHA	PLUNGERS
ATTIC	FLECKS	CURRENCY	CANTEEN	FEROCIOUS
BAZAAR	PILLAR	RAVEN	LINOLEUM	TRUDGED

House on Mango Street Vocabulary

ANCHOR	LINOLEUM	NIMBUS	CUMULUS	FLATS
HYDRANT	LUXURY	PLUCKED	AUTOMATICALLY	CHANDELIER
BAZAAR	CAPSULES	FREE SPACE	AISLES	FLECKS
BAPTIZE	FEROCIOUS	SURGEON	SLANT	IGNITION
INHERIT	ANNUAL	SLATS	ANEMIC	NAPHTHA

House on Mango Street Vocabulary

RESPONSIBILITY	CONTENT	TRUDGED	CURRENCY	ATTIC
GOBLETS	COMPLICATED	THRESHOLD	INTERN	TWANGY
CANTEEN	DESCENDED	FREE SPACE	PLUNGERS	MARIMBAS
PILLAR	DISTANT	RAVEN	HYSTERICAL	NAPHTHA
ANEMIC	SLATS	ANNUAL	INHERIT	IGNITION

House on Mango Street Vocabulary

CHANDELIER	HYDRANT	AISLES	NAPHTHA	THRESHOLD
ANNUAL	PLUNGERS	GOBLETS	NIMBUS	CURRENCY
DISTANT	ATTIC	FREE SPACE	TRUDGED	BAZAAR
RESPONSIBILITY	FLECKS	SLANT	COMPLICATED	IGNITION
FEROCIOUS	AUTOMATICALLY	STRUTTED	INTERN	TWANGY

House on Mango Street Vocabulary

ANCHOR	PLUCKED	INHERIT	CANTEEN	CAPSULES
ANEMIC	CUMULUS	RAVEN	CONTENT	DESCENDED
BAPTIZE	SLATS	FREE SPACE	LINOLEUM	PILLAR
HYSTERICAL	LUXURY	FLATS	MARIMBAS	TWANGY
INTERN	STRUTTED	AUTOMATICALLY	FEROCIOUS	IGNITION

House on Mango Street Vocabulary

PILLAR	INTERN	PLUCKED	LINOLEUM	AUTOMATICALLY
DISTANT	MARIMBAS	SURGEON	ATTIC	CHANDELIER
CURRENCY	CANTEEN	FREE SPACE	DESCENDED	STRUTTED
COMPLICATED	RAVEN	NIMBUS	TRUDGED	TWANGY
HYSTERICAL	ANCHOR	SLANT	LUXURY	AISLES

House on Mango Street Vocabulary

BAPTIZE	IGNITION	THRESHOLD	FLATS	BAZAAR
FEROCIOUS	NAPHTHA	RESPONSIBILITY	FLECKS	CONTENT
INHERIT	CAPSULES	FREE SPACE	PLUNGERS	ANEMIC
SLATS	GOBLETS	HYDRANT	CUMULUS	AISLES
LUXURY	SLANT	ANCHOR	HYSTERICAL	TWANGY

House on Mango Street Vocabulary

PLUNGERS	CUMULUS	RAVEN	DISTANT	AUTOMATICALLY
LUXURY	COMPLICATED	CONTENT	AISLES	THRESHOLD
HYSTERICAL	SLANT	FREE SPACE	NIMBUS	HYDRANT
CHANDELIER	FLECKS	IGNITION	CURRENCY	CAPSULES
SURGEON	MARIMBAS	LINOLEUM	ATTIC	GOBLETS

House on Mango Street Vocabulary

CANTEEN	BAPTIZE	ANEMIC	STRUTTED	RESPONSIBILITY
TEMPORARY	TWANGY	SLATS	INHERIT	ANNUAL
PLUCKED	TRUDGED	FREE SPACE	PILLAR	BAZAAR
FLATS	ANCHOR	NAPHTHA	DESCENDED	GOBLETS
ATTIC	LINOLEUM	MARIMBAS	SURGEON	CAPSULES

www.ingramcontent.com/pod-product-compliance
Lightning Source LLC
Chambersburg PA
CBHW081457070526
44586CB00019B/2401